RATHER ROTTENER

More than 900 *naughty* new limericks

JOHN SLIM

Illustrated by
COLIN WHITTOCK

Foreword by
GYLES BRANDRETH

Published by Underwood Enterprises

Also by John Slim, published by Underwood Enterprises:
**Rotten Haystacks -
More than 870 *new* limericks**

Printed and designed by Cerebus Communications
Published by Underwood Enterprises
47 Alcester Road, Lickey End, Bromsgrove B60 1JT
Telephone & Fax 01527 559221.
ISBN 0-9537613-1-2

CONTENTS

CONTENTS - 2

Page

✲✲✲

FOREWORD

By Gyles Brandreth

THERE was a young lady named Zanka
Who retired while the ship lay at anchor,
    But awoke in dismay
    When she heard the mate say,
"We must pull up the top sheet and spanker."

A limerick, as you probably know, is a five-line nonsense verse that originated with the 18th-century alehouse chorus, *Will you come up to Limerick*. As a form of poetry, it was made famous by Edward Lear.

Although at the limericks of Lear
We may sometimes be tempted to sneer,
    We should never forget
    That we owe him a debt
For his work as the first pioneer.

The trouble with Lear's limericks is that they tend to be remarkably respectable:

There was an old person from Twickenham
Who whipped his four horses to quicken 'em.
    When they stood on one leg,
    He said faintly, "I beg
We may go back directly to Twickenham."

And the trouble with respectable limericks is that they tend to be somewhat short on laughs.

The limerick packs laughs anatomical
Into space that is quite economical,
　　But the good ones I've seen
　　So seldom are clean
And the clean ones so seldom are comical.

Why? Well. . .

The limerick form is complex.
Its contents run chiefly to sex.
　　It burgeons with virgeons
　　And masculine urgeons
And swarms with erotic effects.

As you can tell, I recognise a quality limerick when I see one, but
in truth I hadn't seen that many until I came across the works of
John Slim.

Mr Slim is an extraordinary phenomenon: a distinguished
journalist, a writer of elegant prose; but most of all, best of all,
the Laureate of the Limerick!

He must deserve a place in *The Guinness Book of Records** as
the author of more original limericks than any other writer on
the planet. He deserves a place in *The Oxford Book of Verse* as a
unique poet with a remarkable capacity for encapsulating all
human life in a mere five lines.

Dear reader, in your hands you have one volume of the *War and
Peace* of pint-sized poetry. With its companion volume, *Rotten
Haystacks*, it represents an extraordinary four years' work of the
Tolstoy of rhyme. It is, quite simply, a Slim volume like no other.
Enjoy!

Gyles Brandreth.

---

* Alas for this happy thought, having been confronted by 1,795 brand new limericks in October
1998, the Guinness Editorial Department said that "this was not a category which the editorial
committee decided to monitor." - J S

AUTHOR'S NOTE

The genre's becoming a farce.
New chances of chuckles are sparse.
With no indication
Of much innovation,
It just needs a shot in the arse.

John Slim

INTRODUCTION

Rotten Haystacks *contrived to supply*
Verse guaranteed to comply
With standards and trends
That wouldn't lose friends
At tea with the WI.

This time around, you are faced
With girls who are chased and unchaste;
Bonks, farts and kinks
And out-of-scale dinks
(But in the best possible taste).

These verses, you may have inferred,
Are wilfully wicked, absurd
And neat - but apart
From an arse and a fart,
They don't flaunt a four-letter word.

There's all kinds of verse for your money:
Preposterous, pithy and punny.
There's fun with some nuns,
Some thoughts on the runs.
Alas, they're not clean but they're funny.

***

THE PEOPLE AND PLACES

Appearing in verse in these pages are:

THE PEOPLE

FRED; plus
Adair, Adam, Alice, Andy, Aneurin, Anne, Annie, Bab, Dick
Barton, Battle, Bell, Highwayman Bess, Beverley, Bill, Billy,
Bishop of Birmingham, Blodwen, Bloxwich, Boadicea, Bob,
Bo Peep, Boris, Bottom, Boy Blue, Brahms, Brenda, Bridget,
Bright, Blanche Brightly, Brits, Mrs Brown, Brother Bruce,
Bryn, Caesar, Camilla, the Captain, Carole, Carolina, Chantelle,
Charles, Charlie, Prince Chas, Chatburn, Cinders, Sister Clare,
Clive, Cold Casanova, Viscount Cobham, Cook, Mrs Crapper,
Thomas Crapper, Crockett, Jacques de la Croix, Cupid, Cyril,
Dad, Daddy, Dan, Daphne, Daughter, Dawn, Dean of St Paul's,
Dick, Donald, Ben Doon, Stud Dove, Duchess, the Duchess of
York, the Duke, Eros, Evan, Eve, Ezekiel, Fay, Sarah Ferguson,
Fifi, Fox, Fran, Fruity, G & S, Geoff, Georgina, Gervaise, Glad,
Gladys, Hamlet, Harold, Hopalong Goldberg, Grandpa, Granny,
a Greek, Gus, Hannah, Barren Hardup, Heather, Heep, the Heir
to the Throne, Hilda, Miss Howard, Imelda, Izzy, Jack, Jacquelyn,
James, Jane, Janet, Jean, Jill, Jilly, Jim, Sister Jo, Joan, Joanne,
Jock, Joe, Brother John, Jones, Josh, Don Juanabe, Jude, Julie,
K G, Karen, Kate, Kay, the King, Kit, Leda, Linda, Liszt, Little
Bo Peep, Lois, Louise, Luton Girls' Choir, Phil McCavity, Ma,
Mabel, the Maid of Orleans, Man, Mandy, Sister Marie, Mark,
Mary, David Mellor, Sister Mercy, Michael, A A Milne, Miranda,
Mommy, Mona Lisa, Morag, Morgan, Mother, Miss Muffet,
Mum, Mummy, Nan, Nature, Mother Nature, Nell, Nelly, Willie
Nelson, Nero, Nick, Nye, Old Harold, Paddy, Pat, Patricia, Paul,

Penelope, Penny, Pete, Petunia, Pickem, Plantem, Polly, Pooh, the Pope, Marco Polo, Elvis Presley, Price, the Queen, Rebecca, Rex, King Richard, Rick, Rhoda, Rise-and-Shine, Rob, Roger, Rover, Roy, Roz, Rudolph, Russ, Sally-Jane, Sam, Samuel, Sandy, Santa, Sean, Shakespeare, Sharon, Shefali, Sid, Snowy, Spooner (the Rev), Steph, Stoker, Sue, Susan, Susie, Lady Sybil, Ted, Great-Uncle Ted, Tess, Thamantha, Thomas, Thor, Thrupp, Tina, Desmond Tinnie, Titania, Todd, Tom, Tommy, Tracy, Trevor, Friar Tuck, the Ugly Sisters, Venus, Leonardo da Vinci, Viv, Wallis, Wanda, Wayne, Wendy, Wibble, Wicket, Zeus.

THE PLACES

Abergavenny, Aberystwyth, Australia, Baghdad, the Bahamas, Bali, Beachy Head, Belize, Bicester, Birmingham, Blaby, Boulogne, Brum, Bude, Bute, Caerphilly, Carlisle, Chard, Cheam, China, Clee, Clovelly, Clun, Clwyd, Crete, Crewe, Crickhowell, Cymstrotha, Delph, Devizes, Devon, De Witts, Diss, Dorking, Dorset, Dover, Dundee, Dunoon, Eagle and Trumpet, Ealing, East Sheen, Eltham, England, Epsom, Fareham, Fife, Filey, Finsbury Park, Florence, France, Gibraltar, Gillingham, Gloucester, The Gower, Graceland, the Grand, Gwent, Hampton Loade, Haseley, Haseley Knob, Hay, Hong Kong, Iraq, Kent, Kerry, Kincaid, Knots Landing, Leek, Leicester, Linlithgow, Looe, Luton, Madrid, Mafeking, Maine, Manchester, Nantes, Old Trafford, Oz, Paisley, Palma, Penang, Pipe Hayes, Pisa, Poole, Purley, Qatar, Rabat, Rhyl, Rio, Rome, Rouen, Ryde, St Mawes, St Paul's, Salop, Samoa, Sark, Sarum, Scillies, Senegal, Shropshire, Smite, Soho, South Arkansas, South Bengal, South Borehamwood, Southend, South Tyne and Wear, Spain, Spello, Sri Lanka, Stavanger, Stoke, Stroud, Suez, Tal-y-llyn, The Sun, The Weald, The Wyke, Tonypandy, Torbay, Torquay, Tring, Troon, Turin, Upton Park, Uranus, Valletta, Verdun, Victoria, Villa Park, Wall, Ward J, Westminster Cathedral, Wick, Wickham, Wigwig, Woking, The Wold, Yonkers, Zed.

FRED

It's Fred who will frequently hold
Centre-stage in the tales we unfold -
And in recognition
Of limerick tradition,
He's randy, rumbustious and bold.

These saucy adventures he's led
Have not always typified Fred.
So if you'd prefer the
Pure, go no further:
Just buy *Rotten Haystacks* instead.

A HEALTH WARNING

Repetitive metrical flow
Could well drive you bonkers, and so
It wouldn't be clever
For you to endeavour
To read this small book in one go.

***

I
SPORTING GESTURES

S ome naturists, camping near Wick,
Established a communal trick.
    One lay on the ground
    And rapidly found
The others played quoits with his dick.

    West Ham, Crystal Palace - a sparse
    Chance of a soccer-based farce:
        The start of each name,
        And Arsenal's the same,
    Together will make, *We cry arse!*

The cricket club groundsman, old Clive,
Shown mounds on the pitch (there were five),
    Said, "We keep getting moles
    But I bung up the holes
And bury the buggers alive."

    Rowing's a curious sport: a
    Cox gives us oarsmen no quarter.
        Just keeps us all rowing,
        Can't see where we're going.
    If we win, throw the sod in the water.

Tina's tennis has earned her renown,
With a smash that's the talk of the town.
    Her free-flowing chest
    Is seen at its best,
Going up when she's on her way down.

Sporting Gestures

. . . helps to protect genitalia

Sporting Gestures

Batsmen are often a failure
In England, Sri Lanka, Australia.
    But they all keep their cocks
    And their rocks in a box,
Which helps to protect genitalia.

    A young racing driver said part
    Of the fun of his marital art
        Is to get pole position
        And come to coition
    With the thrust of a good standing start.

A tennis girl's fans were unnerved
By her farts at the moment she served.
    But now she is artless
    And fault-free and fartless,
And corked where it can't be observed.

    Said a sheepish young sheila from Oz,
    "I dreamed I was with my friend Roz,
        In a crowd-pleasing streak
        At the Test Match last week -
    And then I woke up and I was."

A well-endowed lady in tears
Had skipped in the nude several years,
    But still got a shock as
    Her marvellous knockers
Flew up with a clip round the ears.

    A gay wing three-quarter called Joe
    Said, "I do like the game, even though
        My hopes to play forward
        Have all been ignorward
    Since the time I upset the front row."

15

Sporting Gestures

With a mixed-doubles lady from Wall,
Her chest is what umpires recall.
    She serves and it swings,
    And is called many things -
Double fault, the least likely of all.

    A rugger lad's lass said, "No wonder
    My friends said our match was a blunder.
        When we score, he shouts, 'Try!'
        And he's never said why
    Every try needs so much up-and-under."

The Centre Court gallery groaned
When Boris went down as if stoned.
    He'd omitted to swerve
    From a fast-rising serve.
"New balls, please", the umpire intoned.

    Said a naturist golfer from Tring,
    "In the rough, in the buff is the thing.
        One never recalls
        Such accessible balls,
    Nor quite so much freedom of swing."

Said the duchess, "I hear oarsmen share
A practice accomplished with flair.
    This means, when they've won,
    They add to the fun
By holding their cocks in the air."

    A one-legged workman from Wick
    Swam the Channel stark-naked, quite quick,
        Expecting encores
        And praise and applause.
    Instead, people said, "Clever dick."

Sporting Gestures

It's horses for courses, they say!
It's horses for courses - hooray!
    When horses for courses,
    The reason, of course, is
They're making new horses that way.

    The nudist club boss sent a fax
    To each member, explaining, "Relax!
        For the sack race we'll hold
        On our sports day, I'm told,
    We'll use plastic clear see-through sacks."

Aged six, Fred was painful to watch
Playing football: he made such a botch
    Of getting the ball.
    We shall always recall
How he headed his dad in the crotch.

* * *

II
LITERARY
LEANINGS

THROUGHOUT *A Midsummer Night's Dream,*
Things aren't really quite what they seem.
    Titania's ass
    Is a bit of a gas:
She's been Pucked and her Bottom's the theme.

Being deaf, and with strange peccadilloes,
While K.G. wove a world in the willows,
    A.A. Milne one day said,
    "I shall place Pooh in bed,
As a sequel to *Wind in the Pillows.*"

THE LIMERICK

Limericks, from time immemorial,
Have established a proprietorial
        Claim on perversions
        And animadversions
And lines by and large lavatorial.

One way that such verses will rivet is
With news of man's penile proclivities
        And careful attention
        To pubic pretension,
Scale, shape, habits, length and activities.

Literary Leanings

When a full house hears Hamlet intone,
"To be or not. . ?" I just groan.
　　How can this pillock
　　Pretend to solillock-
wise when he isn't alone?

　　An Olympian lecher called Zeus*
　　Found a lady called Leda to geus.
　　　　You might say it's not on,
　　　　Being goosed by a swan -
　　But with Zeus on the leus, what's the eus?

> 　　　　* Zeus, or Jupiter, in various disguises, is
> 　　　　prominent in Greek and Roman mythology.

Midsummer Night's Dream is the play
Which is gay (meaning happy). . . and gay.
　　You have to be wary
　　Because there's a fairy
With bottom fixation, they say.

　　A randy young poet from Hay
　　Combines work and pleasure, they say.
　　　　A floozie called Susie
　　　　Will use his Jacuzzi
　　And then be his lay for the day.

A ribald young poet from Tring
Had a brief, unremarkable fling.
　　　　"How", he enquired,
　　　　"Can a man feel inspired,
When cleavage won't rhyme with a thing?"

✳ ✳ ✳

III
ALL FOR ART

A flatulent oaf made a start
On creating an artisan's art.
    He breezed like a vulture
    Through temples of culture:
Work of art, wind of change, worker fart.

    Make a farce of your art - that's the way
    Modern artists make fortunes today.
        Brick-ends, rusting scrap,
        Almost any old crap:
    They farce-art about and we pay.

A *pas de deux's* clearly rehearsed
To finish before his tights burst.
    But it's such a surprise
    When she spreads wide her thighs
And gets carried off, fanny first.

    The smile of the coy Mona Lisa
    Is because Leonardo could plisa.
        The daring da Vinci
        Would give her a pinci,
    Or pata da assa and squisa.

The art we could most do without
Is the art that the smart-arses tout.
    With talent that's sparse,
    They make art a farce,
Just by farce-arting about.

All for Art

. . .wind of change

All for Art

A male ballet dancer wears gear
That intrigues from the front and the rear.
    When you view from the back,
    You see right up his crack -
Yet his bollocks are never that clear.

    A male ballet dancer's no chump. He
    Struts round the stage with a lump he
        Puts on display.
        It's the *Cor! de ballet.*
    (*Encore*, once they've had rumpy-pumpy).

A cheeky young chap on the halls
Always rolls round the stage on his balls -
    Achieving a trick, you'll a-
    gree, so testicular,
There isn't much else one recalls.

    The popular panto, *Aladdin*,
    Is the one Mother Nature goes mad in.
        Widow Twankey, it's known,
        Has no boobs of her own,
    While her son has unmasculine paddin.

A Shakespeare thesp from Crickhowell
Said, "I shit when I'm taking a bowel.
    Curtain calls on first nights
    Involve me and my tights
And a stage-hand with bucket and trowel."

    A mellow young fellow in Spello
    Likes to say, "Come and play on my cello."
        What he means is his dong,
        Which is 12 inches long,
    Sports warts and looks terribly yellow.

IV

MUSICAL ITEMS

FRENCH horns very largely devote
Their lives to strange habits. We note:
They like, it is clear,
A tongue up their rear
And somebody's fist down their throat.

Rome's burning and there in the middle
Is Nero's great musical riddle.
As a hit, he's a myth!
He's just taking the pyth!
They've not yet invented the fiddle.

HIDDEN CHIMES

**Pop singers have trouble requiting
Written words with the sounds they're reciting.
They howl *Ah*, meaning *I* -
Which is, of course, why
Composers don't write about fighting.**

**Examples are frequent, not sparse,
Of singers, whose speech is a farce,
Howling *"Ah!"* meaning *I*,
And *"Wah!"* meaning *Why*.
Wipe your eyes involves wiping your arse.**

Musical Items

I'm musically out in the cold.
My knowledge has not been extolled
    Since I told my friend Joe
    That as far as I know
Willie Nelson's a wrestling hold.

    At a concert, a fellow called Jones
    Blew a fart which defied no-go zones.
        With one slight deflection,
        It played the string section,
    French horn and a brace of trombones.

A lad who does musical farts
Augments local choirs with his arts.
    His particular trick
    Is duets with his dick,
Which whistles the difficult parts.

    Purveyors of pop somehow bring
    Adulation when having a fling.
        And they don't need a voice
        For the job of their choice,
    As most of the buggers can't sing.

Said Liszt to his friend, "I've no qualms
If the future recalls Liszt and Brahms,
    But should it insist
    That we're Brahms and Liszt,
I'll rave from the grave, up in arms."

    A young lady harpist from Rio
    Made friends through a musical trio.
        Lads seeking a pluck
        On her instrument struck
    A chord and she joined them *con brio*.

Musical Items

. . . Willie Nelson

Musical Items

A musical condom* has been
Introduced on the love-making scene.
    It sees you all right
    With *All through the night*
And stands up for *God, save the Queen.*

* Invented in 1996 by a Hungarian painter,
Ferenc Kovacs.

A musical bimbo from Brum
Found fame and acclaim on the drum.
    It was mind-blowing stuff
    When she stripped to the buff
For *bum-titty-bum-titty-bum.*

A songstress who did it for fun,
Also stripped, Friday nights down The Sun.
    She delighted the locals,
    Apart from her vocals,
But kept the day job as a nun.

✻✻✻

V
CURSORY
NURSERY

WHEN Jill climbs the hill, without fail,
Young Jack is right there on her tail.
   And as Jill is sporty,
   She lets Jack be naughty.
He always leaves cash in the pail.

   Little Bo is a scurrilous creep
   Who came home with none of her sheep.
      She'd not lost the bleaters:
      She'd sold them for meat as
   The man with the knife said, "Don't peep."

It sounds just a bit like hard porn
That keeps young Boy Blue in the corn.
   It's better than no job:
   His day job's a blow job,
With sheep and Bo Peep and the horn.

   Hey diddle diddle, the cat
   And the fiddle, or something like that.
      The action moves now
      To a moon-jumping cow.
   The poet was clearly a prat.

There once was an old woman who
Lived all bemused in a shoe.
   She was somewhat distraught,
   With more kids than she ought,
As she didn't know what she should do.

27

Cursory Nursery

Miss Muffet declared, looking glum,
"It's sad, but some lads are quite dumb.
Though it's great in the corn
When Boy Blue gets the horn,
Jack Horner just sticks in his thumb."

Little Red Riding Hood's meeting
At the house of her gran takes some beating.
If a wolf's in your bed,
You must not be misled,
If he's not there for screwing but eating.

VI

THE WORLD
OF WORDS

DIRTY jokes have no future at all.
Their appeal is beginning to pall.
    According to rumour,
    For lavatory humour,
The writing is now on the wall.

    With an honesty long overdue,
    An *auberge* in which scruples are few -
        Where you meet and then spend
        A dirty weekend -
Has now been renamed *Randyvous*.

There's a strange (but not singular) glee
Involved with the term, *Royal We*.
        When out somewhere rural,
        Does one pause for a plural
Behind a convenient tree?

    Initiative? Always as bit
    Out of reach of Georgina and Kit.
        They did get, one day,
        Three-parts of the way -
And landed themselves initiat.

A Senegal girl thought it odd
When her fellow ran off, crying "Sod!"
    He returned the next day
    For a tentative lay.
That's the tale of the Senegal prod.

The World of Words

A penniless Scotsman called Rob
Pawned his kilt while in search of a job.
    He moved south from Paisley
    And travelled through Haseley.
It's now known as Haseley Knob.

    A mistress may show great resource
    In romps in the heather or gorse.
        She's normally seen
        As coming between
    A mister and mattress, of course.

A lad who made love in a camper
Was accustomed to come at a scamper.
    At first she tried harder
    To dampen his ardour -
And later to arden his damper.

    Eros, it's clear, knows the score:
    "I'm Eros, not Queeros!" he'll roar.
        He declines with a shout
        To be buggered about.
    Being laid back to front makes him sorE.

A poor little fellow called Morgan
Had a wife who was known as a gorgon.
        She'd loudly proclaim,
        "He's got the right name:
Capital M and small organ."

    An expert who came from Gibraltar, he
    Explained all the signs without falter. He
        Said, "Infants in infancy
        Don't fear some contingency
    Like anxious adults in adultery."

The World of Words

What kindness is Nature bestowing,
As man does his to-ing and fro-ing!
    Sperm is white, urine's yellow:
    This ensures that a fellow
Knows whether he's coming or going.

ALPHABETICALLY SPEAKING

Alphabetically speaking, you may
Be certain that *night* follows *day*;
    That *spring* precedes *summer*
    And *leak* precedes *plumber*,
And *grass* is what comes before *hay*.

Age before *beauty* is neat,
And *life* after *death* sounds a treat.
    Ten after *nine*
    After *eight* all sounds fine,
But *radish* foreshadows *repeat*.

Turd is a word that is ripe
For lexicographical hype.
    Its position is plain:
    It's just after *strain*,
Habitually followed by *wipe*.

Sex is so short; what is more,
It's followed by *smoke* and then *snore*.
    And, gilding the lily,
    Vagina's near *willy*,
And *bonk's* after *bed*, as of yore.

THE SONG OF CELIBACY

Celibate: adj. *unmarried, single, bound not to marry* - The Shorter Oxford Dictionary.

Celibate - haven't you heard? -
Is a very misunderstood word.
> It holds not a hint
> Not to bonk with a bint,
But means you don't MARRY the bird.

The celibate state, one could say,
Doesn't mean what you've thought that it may.
> If you play it quite brightly,
> And fornicate nightly,
But don't tie the knot, you're OK.

Said a priest, "I am celibate, faced
With the need to be single, not chaste.
> And so, although single,
> I dangle my dingle,
And don't let a gift go to waste."

A shag-happy celibate said,
"Of course I am busy in bed!
> Have you not heard?
> This much-abused word
Merely means that I haven't got wed."

Said a celibate cricketer who
Went out every night for a screw,
> "It's good to be able
> To keep up my label,
My pecker and scoring-rate, too."

There's a bonhomous bishop who said,
"What celibate means is not wed.
> It's a sin and absurd

The World of Words

To marry a bird:
Just give her a bonking instead."

A handsome young gentleman, built
Like a tank, has no feelings of guilt.
  He sees widows' weeds
  And he sorts out their needs:
"Wilt thou?" - and they usually wilt.

There's something that isn't worth chancing:
If you feel your *libido* advancing,
  Tell your partner, "No more!" -
  And get off the floor. . .
What sort of a prat would come dancing?

A peculiar title is Brit.
It's more of a miss than a hit.
  When Brits go abroad,
  They are largely deplored:
It's lucky that *Brit* rhymes with *shit.*

Interrupting the act has a fault
That upsets any lad worth his salt.
  With his humps getting faster,
  It's sudden disaster:
He'd much rather grind to a halt.

"Reproduction's a word", murmured Jane,
"That I hope you will let me explain.
  My recent seduction
  By Fred caused production.
The *re's* when he does it again."

The World of Words

Curvaceous young ladies are full
Of whiles and beguilement and bull.
They manage this better
When wearing a sweater,
And pull your eyes over the wool.

Scruple's a word that is full
Of unchronological bull.
Any lad would know few
Affairs where a screw
Has somehow preceded the pull.

Many a lad is a wannabe.
We say we don't know what they're gonnabe.
A bright one rejoins,
With a lump in his loins,
That his standing right now is Don Juanabe.

A MULTI-RHYMED LIMERICK

Terse verse causes pauses in sin,
When men assay lay in Turin.
They're there, waiting mating,
And stand hating waiting:
Smart tart, verses, curses, thin grin.

Sex-mad but sterile, she hired
Young men who would poke as desired.
Intercourse meant *Hooray!*
In the course of a lay.
Barren Hardup's the name she acquired.

The World of Words

In vain, she had sat on the loo.
Seized up - a crap long overdue.
      Her mother cried, *"Still?*
      I reckon you're ill!"
She answered, "Still! Motionless, too!"

A flat-chested duchess who's witless,
Took a letter and scared herself shitless.
      It gnawed at her vitals
      To have more than titles.
She added an *S* and got titless.

A letters exchange is the way
For people who live for the day
      To apply their technique
      To the screwing they seek,
And happily dive for the lay.

An item* began to amuse
Observers who learned they could use
      A meaning they'd missed:
      Not a thing on a list,
A pair held together by screws.

* A curious term which arrived in 1994, meaning a partnership,
probably of a sexual nature.

Said an odious fellow from Crewe,
"There aren't many citizens who
      Are ready or fit
      For my shafts of wit."
He thought we agreed. (We said, "Phew!")

The World of Words

A young keep-fit novice in Brum,
At reading instructions was dumb.
　　To "go for the burn",
　　　Goosed the whole class in turn.
He thought he'd read, "Go for the bum."

A passionate couple in Yonkers
Made love where the youngsters played conkers.
　　When one little lad
　　　Said he thought they were mad,
They replied, "No, we're not - we're just bonkers."

A TWO-IN-ONE
LIMERICK

You keep two-in-one verse alive
By moving lines one, two and five -
　　Exchanging, what's more,
　　Line three with line four,
And hoping some sense will survive.

A wizened old spinster, who knew
Her chances of getting a screw,
　　Made sure that she fed
　　The right clues in bed,
Precisely at quarter-to-two.

Precisely at quarter-to-two,
A wizened old spinster, who knew
　　The right clues in bed,
　　Made sure that she fed
Her chances of getting a screw.

. . . go for the bum.

The World of Words

When in Cornwall and too full of whisky,
It might be thought rude and be risky,
    To suggest a loo door
    Can't be opened before
You find out who's hidden the pisky.

    Miss Howard asked, "Is this the norm?"
    When she saw her first dink in the dorm.
        She was so unelated,
        She later created
    Her own League for Penile Reform.

A charming young fellow from Bute
Had a way with his words which was cute.
    He said, "As a rule,
    When I fart, I flatule,
And I don't have a wash - I ablute."

    "On this", Jack declared, "please depend:
    I will lay down my wife for a friend."
        But Jill said to Jock,
        "How big is your cock?
    I'd hate to be at a loose end."

A bird with big bristols once said,
"Is is likely that life might have led
    My chest to have chesters
    Or lincolns or leicesters
Or swanseas or cardiffs instead?"

    No woman's been known to refuse
    To go with a friend to the loos
        And line up in force -
        With handbags, of course -
    While minding their pees and their queues.

VII

ANARCHIC
ANAGRAMS

CONSERVATION'S concerns were extended
In a message to Greenpeace, amended
   By an anagram bore:
   Protect *seal shore*
Made arseholes the things they defended.

David Mellor* could not be ignored,
Although there were few who'd applaud.
   One time he was bold,
   Viscount Cobham was told,
"Well, ain't he *a devil, m'lord!*"

> * David Mellor, MP, who resigned as Heritage
> Minister after publicity over his affair with an
> actress, was later revealed to be having an
> affair with Lady Penelope Cobham, of Hagley
> Hall, Worcestershire.

Sarah Ferguson* sure didn't give a damn:
She got fun in the sun - you were topless, Ma'am:
   A toe-sucking clanger
   (And right royal anger)
And *Fun so rash (rage)* as her anagram.

> * The world's press carried sensational photographs of
> Sarah Ferguson, Duchess of York, enjoying a break with
> her financial adviser.

Anarchic Anagrams

Marco Polo*, it seems, was a chap
Who found he could not read a map.
    With deceitful intent,
    He pretended he went
To China - and so. . . *Loom, O crap!*

G & S - THE TRUTH

G and S, you might guess, were aglow
With an anagram made of *The Yeo-*
        men of the Guard,
        On which they'd worked hard:
They do me one HUGE fart! Good show!

The tasteless is clearly no bar
Elsewhere in their famed repertoire.
        There's *Thespis.* What's this?
        It's taken *The piss.*
Princess Ida? Oh, she's *Pissed in car.*

Gondoliers (with a definite article)
Hired gents' loo (not at all D'Oyly Carticle).
        And see how they've chosen
        A link with *The frozen*
Captain pees for *Penzance* (the Pirarticle).

A ship for men - did you know? -
Is *HMS Pinafore.* So
        They clearly rehearsed
        An anagram first,
And then found a name for a show.

40

Anarchic Anagrams

Him Tarzan? We doubt it a bit.
His much-reviled book was a hit -
    But grassing up Di
    Is probably why
James Hewitt's* *Me J - a wet shit.*

> * James Hewitt, an Army officer, was widely castigated
> after the appearance in 1994 of his book containing kiss-
> and-tell allegations about the Princess of Wales.

Lusting lads always wanted to meld 'em,
But the answer they got quickly quelled 'em.
    They could tell by those toddles
    That the girls were all models -
But models get changed and say *seldom.*

If his willy won't rise, there's dismay.
Not much he can do, one could say.
    If that's all he's got,
    Putting *penis* in *slot*
Makes it *pointless* to have it away.

VIII
A SLIP OF THE TONGUE

IF your tongue isn't slick, don't say quickly
A phrase in which traps are laid thickly.
    Friar Tuck, pheasant plucker,
    Just waits for a sucker
To end with a grin that is sickly.

    In the bathroom, the duke had a fit:
    Pulled the plug, dropped his ring, that was it.
        In the town sewage works,
        The prospect of perks
    Spurred fifty-six sifters of shit.

***

IX

REVERSALS

CRAPPY RUBSNIFF! You're left in the dark?
Say it backwards then, just for a lark.
    Upton Park gives a clue:
    In reverse, *Crap not poo.*
The other one's Finsbury Park.

    A thoughtful transsexual said, "Nurse!
    My death will be life in reverse!
        Life, with my whims,
        Has been all hers and hims.
    My death will be all hymns and hearse."

Manchester finds with a start,
On learning the back-to-front art,
    That - lo and behold! -
    Old Trafford's not old,
But merely old doctor of fart.

    The grounds of the Claret-and-Blue
    In reverse are a terrible two.
        Does Villa Park strive
        To become *crap alive?*
    Does Upton Park choose crap *not poo?*

✳✳✳

X

IMPERFECTLY CORRECT

ADVOCATES of PC thought we might
Think *gingerbread persons** all right.
    They thought they would risk it,
    Thus taking the biscuit:
There wasn't a willy in sight.

> * In January 1994, staff of a West Country supermarket
> relabelled all its gingerbread men "gingerbread persons."
> And in 1997, members of the Aberdeenshire Federation of
> the Scottish Women's Rural Institute were told to make
> "gingerbread people" for their monthly shows.

Calling actresses actors, though silly,
Is a fad which took fun to Caerphilly.
    The actor Blanche Brightly
    Was greeted twice-nightly
With "Boyo! Now show us your willy!"

The ballcock's* a thing, we now find,
"Nice" plumbers must please leave behind.
    It's clear that PC -
    Absurd, OTT -
Can't cope with its own dirty mind.

> * The ballcock and the grease nipple provoked a flurry of
> predictable indignation from the usual quarters.

Imperfectly Correct

A liberal Ms (not a Mrs)
Asserts that she's certain what blrs:
      It's a unisex loo,
        Where she's paused for a poo,
And a guy stands beside her and prs.

      For panto correctness, we may
      Be faced with the need to display
          The two Ugly Sisters
          As mses, not misters,
      With Cinders a suitable gay.

A salesperson answered an ad:
"I'm neither a lass nor a lad.
      I'm what you'd expect,
        With no sex but correct,
And that's why I've never been had."

          ✳✳✳

XI

OLD
HAROLD

OLD Harold believes diabetes
To be both a curse and a treat: he's
Convinced that he oughta
Use sugar-laced water -
And pisses each day on his wheaties.

Old Harold believes diarrhoea
Is two words whose meaning's quite clear.
The first, epithetical,
Describes the pathetical
State of the second one, *rear.*

Old Harold believes that short-sighted
Is all about bowels that aren't blighted.
One sort, constipated,
Just waited and waited -
And meanwhile, the other sort shited.

Old Harold believes time and motion
Is something to do with the notion,
When bowels are slow,
Or don't even go,
How quicker they are with a potion.

Old Harold, on elbows and knees,
Went and bonked some baboons in Belize.
He told them coition
Took place on condition
The children were raised as RCs.

Old Harold

Said Harold, "The trouble with sex
Is how many evenings it wrex.
    If I lie on my belly
    In front of the telly,
The missus says, "'England expex. . .'"

    Old Harold tried hard to explain
    To a bimbo he'd met on a train,
        As he lay there in bed
        With his thing to her head,
    That he'd heard she had sex on the brain.

Old Harold's technique is quite handy,
Whenever he's eager and randy.
    When they've met once or twice, it is
    Sod all the niceties.
Foreplay is buying a shandy.

    Old Harold these days tends to make
    His birthday an annual mistake.
        It's the way that he handles
        The quenching of candles
    By pissing all over the cake.

Old Harold's now drawing his pension
And often finds reason to mention
    That now and again,
    His bladder and brain
Show similar lack of retention.

    Old Harold's a pain when he's pissed.
    He's known to be prone to insist
        On shouting out, *"Snap!"*
        Or similar crap,
    When the aim is a plain game of whist.

XII
LOGICAL
LAPSES

There are suddenly no signs at all
Of flies on the dining room wall.
    It shows we were right,
    Putting buckets of shite
In the sitting room, kitchen and hall.

    Mrs Crapper's* inaugural piddle
    Made a mess, although solving a riddle.
        Tom then prevented
        Distress: he invented
    A seat with a hole in the middle.

* Thomas Crapper was the Victorian plumbing
pioneer who patented a device which gave
"a certain flush and an easy pull."

A lady who shops in the nude
Says a benefit which has accrued
    Is that, viewed in the buff,
    She is seen as quite rough,
So that clothed, she's not stalked or pursued.

    "Waiter! You haven't a clue!
    Your thumb's in my soup!" "Sir, I knew.
        Out here, that's the norm:
        It keeps my thumb warm.
    In the kitchen, it's up my arse, too."

XIII

SIGNS OF UNCERTAINTY

THE *R* has been changed to a *P*,
So the public seeks pissoles for tea.
Says the shopkeeper, "Bah!
That *P* should be *R!*"
Says the public: *"R-soles? Give us three!"*

It's a sign of the times, and it shows
Alongside our roadsides in rows:
Pick Your Own! What excitement!
Non-specific incitement!
Is it teeth, winners, moment or nose?

A signwriter, thinking he knew it all
For a sex shop, could easily screw it all.
One more *L*, then a *D*
Where they'd wanted a *C*,
And *COITAL* soon becomes Do It All.

I think we should all raise our glasses
To flags of convenience farces -
To lavatories labelled
Men, Women, Disabled
In matchsticks and circular arses.

When tarts in Madrid take a stroll,
Their business goes out of control.
Olé in big letters
All over their sweaters
Does wonders for trade on the whole.

Signs of Uncertainty

At the trade fair, old Chatburn looked glum.
He thought it a shame that he'd come.
     A label displayed
     His name and it made
Other visitors call him Chatbum.

     To slow down the mad speeding chumps,
     The road had a series of bumps,
          But brothel confusion
          Arose from profusion
     Of signs saying, *"Watch out for humps."*

Said Fred, "What's the point of denial?
I simply don't piss with a style
     That meets the designs
     Of the blue-and-white signs
Which keep saying P half a mile."

     On American freeways, the art
     Is to know what the signposts impart.
          Gas Food simply means
          They'll sell you baked beans
     For you to convert to a fart.

A lady who's lovely, though large,
Does her stint as a bint on a barge.
     But she's made the lads wrecks:
     Gratuitous Sex -
That's her sign - means it's all free of charge.

     The nautical brothel ignored
     The view that all nice girls adored
          A sailor. Instead,
          It had harlots in bed
     And a sign saying, *Man Overbawd.*

Signs of Uncertainty

In a greengrocer's shop in the region,
A visiting sex-starved Glaswegian
    Saw a notice which read,
    Loose Swedes, so she said,
"Give me two - and a naughty Norwegian."

✳ ✳ ✳

XIV

ONE FOR THE ROAD

A thoughtful young fellow named Mark
Always drives in reverse in the dark.
 The bastards behind him,
 Who'd otherwise blind him,
Are blinded themselves, so they park.

 Jack-the-lad knew he had to come clean
 About fun and games he had seen:
  He was driving his Ma
  In his steaming-up car
 When footprints appeared on the screen.

An old man's uncertainty showed
With the name he forgot on the road.
  "Unless I am dreamin',
  It's all cock and semen."
It turned out he meant Hampton Loade.

 "My boy friend has habits", said Rhoda,
 "Which put him in fairly bad odour.
  But he'd much rather keep
  Being seen in a sheep
 Than just be seen once in a Skoda.*"

   * Top car, nevertheless, in a 1998 survey.

A starlet explained she had barred a
Persistent young man from her Lada.
  She said, "His technique
  Is not Method or Greek,
And rarely reminds me of RADA."

XV

LIFE ON THE LAND

A farmer enjoyed the Bahamas,
Where the girls simply loved his pyjamas.
    "They see them", he said,
    "And they jump into bed."
That farmer's pyjamas are charmers.

    A labourer down in The Weald
    Molested a pig in a field.
        We'd never have known,
        But his cover was blown,
    'cos the pig took it big and it squealed.

A cowhand from South Arkansas
Ate enough curry for fas.
    All that vindaloo
    Seemed to burn him right through.
His backside became really ras.

    There is a young farmer in Battle,
    With balls made of metal that rattle;
        And his scrotum of glass is
        To ring as he passes
    And warn when he's driving the cattle.

A pig farmer living near Fareham,
Whose friends said his farts used to scare 'em,
    Let rip with a cry,
    Cleaning out every sty
And showering the shit over Sarum.

Life on the Land

. . . no need to worry

Life on the Land

The laird's shooting party looked tame:
No pheasants to shoot - what a shame!
   Then a lady called Jilly,
   The wife of the gillie,
Said, "No need to worry: I'm game."

A farmer who sat on his ass
Twelve hours every day said, "It's crass -
   But ass muscles send a
   Thrill to my gender,
As long as it's eating the grass."

   Said a rancher, "I have a strange fear,
   The bull I've just bought's a bit queer.
     If ever you find me
     With him right behind me,
   You'll know that I've had a bum steer."

In the hay in the barn in the yard,
The farmer told Susie from Chard,
   "Come here, pretty Sue,
   I've a soft spot for you."
She answered, "I'll wait 'til it's hard."

   "I'm dreadfully sorry", Fred cried.
   "My car hit your rooster! It died!
     I'd like to replace it."
     "Well, if you can face it",
   Said the farmer, "the hens are outside."

***

XVI

RELIGIOUS DISORDERS

SAID a wayward old bishop one night, "E-
ven though, long before I grew flighty,
I would preach to the crowds
With my head in the clouds,
I now use my alb as my nightie."

A novice was somewhat dismayed
At learning she had to get laid.
"What's more", said the abbot,
Removing his habbot,
"Holy orders are promptly obeyed."

Spooner (the Rev) ran amok
And endowed with his name, which has stuck,
Conversational lapses.
Consolation perhaps is
He never once met Friar Tuck.

As Spooner (the Rev) was a hit,
Through transposing his words just a bit,
He had to extend
Amends to a friend,
Appalled to be called shining wit.

A bishop, it seems, was the man
Who soon made a maiden called Anne,
With a bit of the other,
A reverend mother.
And that's when his troubles began.

Religious Disorders

The convent's mood started to heat up,
With nuns too excited to eat up,
    When Sister Marie
    (Who'd been for a pee)
Discovered the lavatory seat up.

    A charming old cleric from Bude
    Said, "I hate folks to think I'm a prude.
        I'm really quite gay -
        In an old-fashioned way -
    And I always take baths in the nude."

A bishop, who's had a few drinks,
Observes a young tart as she winks.
    Says the randy old trout,
    "She's about to find out
A bishopric's not what she thinks."

    A randy bisexual punk
    Who screwed the closed orders when drunk
        Said, "I like having fun.
        If there's none with a nun,
    There's a bonk in a bunk with a monk."

With a late urge to breed like a rabbit,
Brother Bruce was reluctant to grab it.
    He'd had years as a monk
    In a celibate bunk
And couldn't get out of the habit.

    A gardener based on a theory a
    Romp with a nun fairly near here.
        I am no fibber:
        He dibbed with his dibber.
    She's now an earth mother superior.

Religious Disorders

The abbot dropped dead as he starred
In a romp with a novice in Chard.
　　　　Said the novice, "I know,
　　　　Having just seen him go,
Why they say that old abbots die hard."

Just WHY did that bishop of Birmingham
Have fun with young girls while confirmingham?
　　　　Kissing his ring
　　　　Did things to his thing,
Then he shot some episcopal spirmingham.

　　　　A bishop, a randy old sod,
　　　　Assiduous servant of God,
　　　　　　With lecherous glee,
　　　　　　Screwed choristers (three).
　　'twas a spree that his see saw as odd.

THREE OF A KIND

There are those who think Fred is disgusting,
But he does want to know,'cos he's busting:
　　　　Which was the mission
　　　　They caught in position,
And which members' members were thrusting?

Missionaries have recognition
For their way of achieving coition.
　　　　They cannot combat it;
　　　　Were clearly caught at it,
In mission coition position.

A missionary said, with a gloat,
"'The Position' was named while afloat.
　　　　I was humping a whore
　　　　When they yelled from the shore,
'Lie down, 'cos you're rocking the boat!'"

Religious Disorders

A misogynist Welshman called Bryn
Dropped dead one dark night in Turin.
    The unfortunate sod
    Said he'd come to see God.
Said the angel, "I'll see if She's in."

RELIGIOUS STRIFE

There's a popular bird called a pigeon,
And another, less known, is a widgeon.
    But they're no bloody use -
    Any more than a goose -
When you need a good rhyme for *religion*.

Religion is what's always stirred
Every horrible thing that's occurred.
    It's the main cause of wars -
    No wonder rhyme's laws
Ensure it keeps getting the bird.

    The most-travelled fart one recalls
    Was unleashed by a dean of St Paul's.
        Without losing spice,
            It went round the world twice,
    Returning to tickle his balls.

A fart with too much compressed air
Surprised a young novice at prayer.
    It shredded her drawers,
    Blew down several doors
And gave passing aircraft a scare.

    The loudest fart ever recorded -
    Brother John's, on a plane, as he boarded -
        De-waxed the crew's ears
        Then drowned all the cheers
    Of passengers as they applauded.

Religious Disorders

A bishop who strayed was annoyed.
As thousands of words were deployed,
    And *entendres* became lewder
    And inference ruder.
Bishop's palace was one to avoid.

    A flatulent nun, Sister Clare,
    Always makes the whole convent aware
        When she turns up for Mass:
        It's a bit of a gas -
    Coming in on a wind and a prayer.

At the mission, the lovely Shefali
Grew large and bore fruit while in Bali.
    The poor little sod,
    While working with God,
Had also been playing with Charlie.

    An incestuous curate's caprice
    Linked his sins with his prayers for release.
        He fashioned his ration
        Of family passion
    Each time he got down on his niece.

A healthy young priest says repression
Disturbs him somewhat in Confession.
    When he's told fleshly sin,
    Such stirrings begin,
He'll rush out to give them expression.

    Two nuns caused a stir at the fete,
    With a decorous strip at the gate.
        They slipped off their wimples,
        Revealing their dimples.
    The curate kept dropping the plate.

Religious Disorders

Said a bishop who strayed, "I declare, it
Is part of my nature to bear it:
      When people protest
      That it's not for the best,
I reply, 'If the mitre fits, wear it'."

      Said the actress, "My lord, that was fine!"
      Said the bishop, "It's surely a sign,
            That I think that yours
            Deserves some encores,
      And you think that mine is divine."

Said a bishop, while having a pee,
"My bishopric does this for me.
      It's an apt name, although,
      While the damn' thing's on show,
I suppose I could call it a see."

      A devilish dirty old druid
      Ensured when he lured girls to Clwyd
            That they got quite a shock
            From under his frock,
      With a squirt of liturgical fluid.

The parish routine caused dismay
For a long-standing reader, they say.
      A series of vicars
      Got into her knickers,
As Tuesdays were lay reader day.

      Said a bishop who bonked, "I'm a blighter
      Who was somewhat constrained by his mitre.
            I had not a hope
            That I'd cope with my cope,
      So I frocked off and learned to delight her."

Religious Disorders

A novice enquired, "As I'm chaste,
Does it means I am seen as disgraced,
      Since the chasing is done
      By a lesbian nun
And an abbot I've so far outpaced?"

      A curate who went on a spree,
      When in bed with a call girl, said, "We
            Have never rehearsed,
            So tell me the first
      Of the options now open to me."

Sister Clare, with a coy little snigger,
Said, "The squits are quite good for the figure.
      But it's nice when they've gone
      And you're back to square one
And can fart with your usual vigour."

      The parish soon grew to depend
      On Aneurin as curate and friend.
            To cheer up the sick,
            He would whip out his dick.
      The bishop warned, "Nye is the end."

Said a randy old canon, "The wits
Are naturally tickled to bits.
      Well, making a pass
      While saying High Mass
Can probably count as the pits."

      The canon declared, "I hate needle
      Re my whang, by rude folks like the beadle.
            The thing they deplore here
            Goes right down Victoria
      And twice round Westminster Cathedral."

Religious Disorders

Supposing, by way of contrition,
A pope who had strayed joined a mission.
What on earth would he say
When, on his first day,
He was asked to describe his position?

To a randy archbishop's delight,
His episcopal whang worked all night.
Within the archdiocese,
This caused quite a criocese,
With ladies beginning to fight.

A hit of a miss called Miranda
Is happy to use her veranda
For tricks she devises
For pricks of all sizes.
The rest of the convent can't stand her.

Said the canon, "I'd always desired
To know at first hand what transpired
When a man sought to mate.
Now I do, and it's great -
But the Pope says I'll have to be fired."

For a pope, life's intriguingly full
Of truths and of pulling the wool:
Infallible teachings
Contained in his preachings -
And just now and then, papal bull.

The novice said, "Though I'm devout,
I know what I'm doing without -
So when I'm aglow,
I let the monks know,
And they're there when I put it about."

Religious Disorders

Said the vicar, "I'm now realising
Why the lads say it won't be surprising,
    On Sundays at least,
    With the new woman priest,
If there's widespread religious uprising."

    The curate is not a bit witty.
    When he sings, it's not pleasant or pretty.
        But he does have recourse
        To a cock like a horse,
    Entertaining the ladies' committee.

The cry of *"Oh, shit!"* was so quick
That Fred ceased to play with his dick,
    Leaping up to abuse
    Sister Clare with his views:
"Don't shout *shit!* in church, you old prick!"

    The Church was unable to cope
    With Pope Joan,* but it gave itself scope
        To prevent a repeat
        With pontifical seat
    With a hole in, for groping the Pope.

* Pope Joan is said to have reigned as Pope
John VIII for two years from 855 until,
according to legend, she was discovered when
she gave birth during a papal procession in
Rome and was then lynched. She is believed to
have been a woman from Dorset. Afterwards, it
is said, the Church provided a chair with a hole
through which a young cardinal would reach
between a papal candidate's vestments to check
that he was a man

XVII
JUST BACK IN TIME

FIRST, the England team coach* turned the knife
And caused the disabled much strife,
   Then, as ex-coach, it's said,
   He was scratching his head,
Contemplating his previous life.

> * Glenn Hoddle lost his job as England football coach in
> February, 1999, after being reported as saying that disabled
> people were paying for the sins of a previous existence.

Monica* said, "I concede a
Point: the White House didn't need a
   Stain on my dress
   For people to guess
I'd been to play swallow-my-leader."

> * The 1998-99 scandal of the relationship between Monica
> Lewinsky, a young White House intern, and US President
> Bill Clinton, led to a report by prosecutor Kenneth Starr.

Boadicea, charioteer: no mistaking.
The knives on her wheels set men shaking.
   They used not to mind
   When they saw her behind -
Just the punctures she caused, overtaking.

I came, saw and conquered. Proclaim
Your successes, O Caesar! The same
   Fundamentals apply
   To his love life: that's why
He saw, she concurred and he came.

XVIII
BIBLICAL BITS

THE Fall of Mankind's down to Adam -
But Eve was a bit of a madam.
 Seeing her and her wares,
 He cried, "Sod it! Who cares?"
Then his fig leaf fell off and he hadam.

 Said Adam, when in at the birth
 Of the sex act, "Now, would it be worth
  My putting this queer
  Thing into your ear?
 It's looking like nothing on earth."

Cried Adam, "I've seen in a vision
Where to place my small pole with precision!"
 Said Eve, "Please believe -
 How I'd grieve to deceive! -
My headache's no conscious decision."

 Adam was ribbed - what a plonker! -
 But thus gained a girl friend to conquer.
  She thought him a freak,
  But he cried, "It's unique!"
 (Raised cain and was abel to bonk her).

Adam rose with a satisfied grin.
"What a curious way to begin!
 To hell with the apple!
 Consider that grapple
A far more original sin."

Biblical Bits

The angel's glad tidings could keep.
Said the shepherds (great joy? *Sound asleep!*):
    "We don't care who you are!
    You can go stuff that star!
Clear off, and stop scaring the sheep!"

    They've said to Ezekiel, "Come off it!"
    He stands on the roof, by the soffit.
        He raves and he rants
        With a hole in his pants,
    And his bottom line showing a prophet.

There's a wonderful wench on The Wold
Whose biblical gown knocks 'em cold.
    Its *décolletage*
    Is the cause, by and large,
Why it's known as the lo and behold.

    A Biblical stripper, Salome,
    Said, "People are getting tanome
        Since Herod said, 'What
        Do you think you have got
    Under wraps that you're willing tashome?'"

***

XIX

THE NATIONAL HEALTH

A dashing young dentist in Kent
Found in practice, wherever he went,
Girls only too willing
To have a good filling:
"Open wide!" stirred their carnal intent.

DIY gynaecologists all
Drive their wives without fail to the wall.
They're the men who,
By reaching in through
The letter-box, paper the hall.

A handsome young dentist in Gillingham
Treats ladies so well that he's thrillingham.
They all give a shout
When he's pulling it out,
And a few will go *Oo!* when he's drillingham

A lesbian said, "It's a shock to me!
How thoughtful and kind can a doctor be!
He says he'll extend a
Help to my gender.
The process is called strapacoctomy."

A horrified son of the soil
Was given no chance to recoil
When he heard a young nurse,
Known to work in reverse,
Being told to start pricking his boil.

The National Health

The impotence drug was refined
Like the organ for which it's designed:
Take it too much in hand,
And you could understand
Why they say that it may send you blind*

* Blindness was given as possible side-effect
when Viagra was introduced in Britain in 1998.

A hopeful young surgeon called Todd
Sawed off someone's head, the poor sod.
This made quite a mess
Of his FRCS:
He had to go through on the nod.

DNA, sad to say, intervenes,
Divorcing the end from the means.
As Jack said to Jill,
Procreation's no thrill
When boffins get into your genes.

Embryology can, it's reported,
Make family trees look distorted.
Poor little laddie!
A test tube's his Daddy -
And Mummy's a foetus (aborted).

* Oh, no she's not! In 1994, the Human Ferti-
lisation and Embryology Authority, which
licenses fertility clinics, banned scientists from
using eggs from aborted foetuses to treat
infertile women.

Propped up in his bed, Fred will start
To lean to one side, then a smart
And attentive young nurse
Sits him up and he'll curse,
"A chap gets no time for a fart!"

The National Health

... my pen's stuck

The National Health

A hospital doctor looked glum,
Then he sighed, to confide in his chum:
    "Thermometer, Crockett,'
    Is here in my pocket.
My pen's stuck up somebody's bum."

    Medical shorthand is very
    Inclined to be brief but quite merry.
        We leave paediatrics
        To be geriatrics:
    As doctors say, pee into jerry.

The love pill soon raised expectations,
Cocks, numbers of bonks, penetrations. . .
    What a great way of proving
    That when the earth's moving,
The Health Service* needs firm foundations!

    * The possible cost of Viagra was put at "billions" in 1998

    Hands-on is the method of healing
    Which girls seem to find most appealing.
        They're never too sure
        They'll emerge with a cure,
    But they know that they'll get a good feeling.

A greedy young fellow from Delph
Bought marital aids off the shelf.
    As soon as he savoured
    His condoms (mint-flavoured),
He thoughtlessly ate them himself.

    With a rectal inspection to come, it a-
    nnoyed him, exposing his bum; it a-
        ppalled him, alerted,
        To find they'd inserted
    A daffodil, not a thermumita.

The National Health

Said a lad with *libido* fixation,
"All I need is a quick consultation.
    Just the thrust of a bust,
    And my lust is a must."
"All you need", said the shrink, "is castration."

    A dissatisfied lady in Bloxwich
    Sent her man for a check to the doxwich
        Eventually led
        To his taking a bed
    In a specialised ward, for a coxwich.

TWO OF A KIND

Though a surgeon named James is quite dim,
His patients speak highly of him.
    It's not that one raises
    One's voice in Jim's praises:
Jim chops off one's balls on a whim.

A surgeon whose home was in Filey
Chopped the balls off young men rather wryly.
    It left them no choice
    About raising their voice,
And explained why they spoke of him highly.

    A patient vouchsafed with dismay
    That a hefty young nurse, name of Kay,
        Grabbed the thing in the middle
        He uses to piddle,
    And carried him off to Ward J.

Although test tube babies aren't rare,
Some girls don't know how to prepare.
    They had to tell Mandy,
    Who's keen, ripe and randy,
"The test tube's not meant to *go there!*"

The National Health

... the thing in the middle

The National Health

"Oh, doctor", cried Fred, "it's not right,
All this wind that I have, day and night.
      What on earth can I do?
      I'm appealing to you."
So the doctor prescribed him a kite.

      A dentist confessed, "I'm obsessed
      With the feel and appeal of a breast.
          Who cares where there's caries?
          A pair in the chair is
      A test of the quest I've suppressed."

A matron whose humour was raw
Would give friends surprises galore.
      If asked, "What's a hospice?",
      She'd scratch her proboscis,
And answer, "Three gallons or more."

      There's a doctor whose minimal dick
      Has caused his syringe-waving trick.
          With designs on the ass
          Of a comely young lass,
      He says, "You'll just feel a small prick."

A handsome young man from Darjeeling
Can do his faith healing with feeling.
      Every girl understands
      That there's joy in his hands,
Though some seem to come for the healing.

      Two lads sat on spikes on a wall.
      The doctor their mum had to call
          Came round to inspect 'em
          And frowned and said, "Rectum?"
      Said their mum, "Did 'em no good at all."

XX

LAWFUL OCCASIONS

SAY police, who've increasingly been
Hosing suspects behind the canteen:
    "If anything's urgent,
    Some caustic detergent
Will soon make the bastards come clean."

    A very tall warder who knew
    He was idle and overweight, too,
        Proclaimed it appalled him
        To learn the lags called him
    A long, slow and comf'table screw.

Said Tracy, whose lad was a copper,
"His truncheon's both hard and a whopper.
    Sharon sees why
    I give it a try -
But Mum thinks it's vaguely improper."

    A young Irish lawyer called Thomas
    Wooed girls in both banking and chomas.
        He said, "Faith and begorrah!
        Oi may be a horrah -
    But Oi'm loikely as not on a phromas."

A lady who showed great resource
With policemen, once murmured, "Of course,
    With quick assignations
    Around police stations,
My life is one long *tour de force.*"

Lawful Occasions

"When Fred's will is read", people said,
"We'll all be surprised" - but instead,
Young Daphne demurred,
"Oh, haven't you heard?
It's normal that Fred's willy's red."

TREATS FOR THE BOYS

The Bench's best joke was to say,
"The prisons aren't working today.
Let's give the yobs fun -
Three weeks in the sun:
The taxpayer-victims will pay."

Don't the judges who laughingly say
A thing that could help crime to pay,
Understand that the victim -
Sod the bastards who kicked him -
Likes criminals out of the way?

***

XXI

ANIMAL ANTICS

A fish in a bowl is a farce.
Its joys may be seen to be sparse,
With a misshapen view
Of people like you,
And a piece of thin string up its arse.

There once was a dear little deer
Who was licking her dear little rear.
She explained, "With some luck,
I shall see a big buck -
And with more luck, the buck will stop here."

Said a bustard, "It's plain to discern,
It would be very easy to earn
(If I were non-U -
Not one *A* but two)
Legitimate cause for concern.

Said a duck, with a cluck, "I don't stress it,
But I'm stuck with my luck and I guess it
Is true that a dove
Rhymes sweetly with *love*,
And a duck with a way to express it."

Whatever makes hedgehogs decide
To winkle their tiggies inside?
One poor little runt
Had a much-punctured front:
His friends knew at once that he'd tried.

Animal Antics

. . . he's had thirty-eights

Animal Antics

When Charlie ran off with a cow,
His wife said, "We've not had a row.
    I think that the glamour is
    Buttercup's mammaries:
He's had thirty-eights until now."

    An animal trainer in Crete
    Had an accident out in the street.
        He got such a bang
        From an elephant's whang.
    He was thoroughly cocked off his feet.

A young cockerel said, "It's dismayed me,
The way Mother seems to evade me.
    It makes me feel fraught:
    Don't you think that she ought
To love me a bit, now she's laid me?"

    My highly intelligent dog
    Tends to turn out a turd like a log.
        But a pea-souper's super
        For hiding a pooper:
    That's perhaps why he craps in a fog.

No wonder a cockerel's not staid;
Is randy, cocksure, unafraid.
    He's never concealed
    He's playing the field:
His first day on earth, he got laid.

    Said a duchess with spots on her bottom,
    "I don't find it easy to spottom,
        But my butler agrees
        That if I've got fleas,
    My bottom's the spot where I've gottom."

... what a bag!

Animal Antics

A convict who filed for divorce
Found his wife was in bed with a horse.
    For the hag - what a bag! -
    To shag with a nag
Was a drag. The lag gagged. It was coarse.

    Said a lady, "It's safer to doodle
    Than get yourself poked by a poodle.
        I'll never get used
        To the brat I produced,
    As its tonsure recalls my canoodle."

When cattle swim rivers, it's clear
Direction's controlled from the rear.
    A cow has its udder
    To use as a rudder.
A bull has what makes it a steer.

    A great tit exclaimed, "It's absurd!
    What a name to inflict on a bird!
        I never protested,
        But should have suggested
    Big bristol was what I preferred."

Your name, little dog, is so apt!
You are sweet. but you ought to be slapped!
    You're known as a shitzu -
    Which certainly fits you,
Considering how you've just crapped.

    Fred, when his bitch was on heat,
    Dipped her backside in petrol - quite neat!
        But a five-year-old lass
        Cried, "She ran out of gas -
    And a dog pushed her right up the street!"

XXII
MARRIAGE LINES

A quick-thinking bridegroom called Ted
Drew a bridesmaid aside as he said,
    "Just slip home with me:
    With your frock off, you'll see
How it matches the drapes on the bed."

    Young women, quite oddly, decide
    To walk up the aisle as a bride.
        Strange way to behave:
        Centre gangway's the nave.
    An aisle is. . . a bit on the side.

Jill's honeymoon hopes had been heightening,
But Jack on the job was quite frightening.
        A vision in Vaseline,
        He just stuck his tassel in
(And-out, in-and-out) like greased lightning.

    So Blodwen is marrying Josh!
    That means that she's pregnant, by gosh!
        Been messing about,
        And is now up the spout!
    She hasn't? She isn't? There's posh!

Fred took his new wife to one side.
"I know", he said, "why you're called *bride*.
        It's easy to see:
        You're a right little b -
As well as a hell of a ride!"

XXIII

DOMESTIC ISSUES

THE answerphone said, "We are out -
Unless an intruder's about:
        In that case, we lurk,
        You burglarous berk.
Lead piping can pack quite a clout."

        I saw one while out on a visit.
        I bought one: it's really exquisite.
                I'm so proud to own
                My new cordless phone -
        But now where the bloody hell is it?

It's always a sad little scene:
Meet a pram and dive under the screen.
        You get no response:
        The babe thinks, "You ponce!
What the hell does *goo-googly-goo* mean?"

        First, pee in an ice tray - don't miss!
        Then place in the freezer. . . like this.
                Though people believe
                It's hard to achieve,
        In the end, it's a sheer piece of piss.

Said a young mum, when out with her brood,
"With this lot, I needn't allude,
        By written confession
        Or public profession,
To having been thoroughly screwed."

Domestic Issues

If anything's hard to forgive, it is
A bathroom bereft of civilities.
    When the seat won't stay vertical,
    You know it will hurt if al-
lowed its cock-chopping proclivities.

    A lonely young man from the Gower
    Would stand on his head in the shower,
        Allowing the spray
        Which came into play
    To play every day for an hour.

A luminous condom's decreed
As the item a fellow may need.
    And according to Fred,
    When he wears one in bed,
And he's under the sheets, he can read.

    In bed in the dark, Fred had grown
    To like his wife's amorous moan.
        He spoiled it one night,
        When he turned on the light
    And found her, mid-moan, on the phone.

A baby, when small, is absurd.
It thinks it should have the last word.
    You're changing its nappy.
    It's not very happy.
It screams, and it won't be deterred.

    Said Sue to her husband, "It's true,
    Fred did to me things which were new,
        And I started to sing
        When in thrall to his thing. . .
    But I never stopped thinking of you."

Domestic Issues

She cried, "Mother's milk is the best!",
While clamping her babes to her chest.
But as she'd had quads,
The poor little sods
Had to get what they could, two a breast.

When Jock dropped his trousers, the shock
Caused Sue to cry, "Coo! Tell me, Jock,
What on earth is that thing
That you keep in a sling,
With its end neatly tucked in one sock?"

Said Fred, "I love Mother, but such
Is life, I'm in jail, out of touch.
I just can't resist her:
She's like a big sister,
Though sex doesn't feature as much."

Their marriage was blissfully based
On carrier bags: one encased
His wife's face and head
While he bonked her in bed;
One was his, in case hers was displaced.

Compatible seems the right label
In the marriage of minds made by Mabel.
It subtly reflects
Her abhorrence of sex
And her joy that her husband's unable.

* * *

XXIV
A LITTLE
LEARNING

PISA'S queer tower was designed
Upright and normal: you'll find
No moral meanings
In unnatural leanings -
Simply the way it's inclined.

Bookshops have such a collection
Of titles, they *can* lose direction.
There on the shelf
Under Do-It-Yourself,
Joy of Sex was awaiting inspection

I require a concise explanation
Of a sex-and-VD situation.
Supposing a chap
Is erect with the clap:
Is he getting a standing ovation?

Increasing the world's population
Calls for convinced copulation
And broody reaction -
Called foetal attraction.
The manual's *The Birth of a Nation.*

"Experience isn't essential",
Said the tart, with an eye to potential.
"My thigh here will serve
As your fast-learning curve,
And everything else is sequential."

A Little Learning

A teacher of maths in Rouen
Considers sex triangles *bons.*
      He chooses his floozies
      As hypotenuses;
Himself, as the square who is on.

      a over *b*, in coition,
      Is multiplication position.
            While maths will divide,
            A screw can provide
      The chance of a little addition.

A student of maths, with a sigh,
Said her tutor was looking too pi.
      "He said it was trig,
      But then it grew big,
And soon it was *x* over *y.*

      Two sex theory courses last winter
      Soon prompted a third course, a splinter.
            Ex-student Petunia
            Says senior and junior
      Got practical back-up through inter.

Despite what some expert decides,
Sex education provides
      No useful improvements
      On well-known youth movements:
It's always boy scouts and girl guides.

      A flatulent fellow called Geoff
      Told his wife, the unfortunate Steph:
            "You know very well
            Why a fart has a smell:
      It's simply an aid to the deaf."

A Little Learning

. . . she counts up to two

A Little Learning

Geography's dealt me a blow.
My favourite "fact" isn't so.
　　Joyous delusion
　　Has gone in confusion!
Florence is not on the Po.

　　Those who resort to coition
　　With little, if any, tuition,
　　　　May find, like this verse,
　　　　That it's brief - and, what's worse,
　　Like this verse, may precede obstetrician.

There's a student of mermaids who begs
Our indulgence awhile as he pegs
　　His research to his need
　　To find how they breed
Without even spreading their legs.

　　At mental arithmetic, few
　　Can stir up excitement like Sue.
　　　　The cheer she arouses,
　　　　Undoing her blouse, is
　　Provoked while she counts up to two.

Here's a thought which may possibly pain us,
Or at least, not do much to sustain us:
　　Did Nature make man
　　For a gap in its plan
That came between penis and anus?

　　Home schooling is very effectual,
　　If an infant's at all intellectual.
　　　　Aged three, little Benny
　　　　Asked Mummy how many
　　Esses to put in *transsexual.*

XXV
MERELY MALES

A laddie who's very well built
Stands out without doubt in a kilt.
    He cannot conceal
    His appeal in a reel,
And a jig goes down big on a stilt.

    With Walkman, all hope disappears
    At the sight of a prat swilling beers
        As he sits on a train,
        With a space for a brain,
    While *ts-ts* comes out of his ears.

When does man start to show some good breeding?
That's not where the first signs are leading.
    As a new human being,
    He spends his time peeing,
Asleep, screaming, puking or feeding.

    Don't scoff at my lack of virility!
    Don't blame me for my infertility!
        Man cannot defy
        Nature - and I
    Inherited Father's sterility.

Sado-masochists' odd little ways
Result in surprising displays.
    A fellow called Rick
    Liked to stand on his prick,
Explaining, "I've done it for daze."

Merely Males

There is a young fellow in Poole,
Whose nickname's been Fruity since school.
His real name is Andy.
It's not that he's randy:
He's got a banana-shaped tool.

A man with a whang with a bend
Talked terms with a tart in Southend.
She said, "Access is fine -
But this one is mine:
It's not for your flexible friend."

A lad with a laughable dong
Had a line that could never be wrong.
With a lass on her back,
Agog for attack,
He would say that it wouldn't be long.

Said a lad with no balls, "None's enough, as
The fillies have found no-one suffers.
It works like a dream:
They bonk at full steam,
And never collide with the buffers."

A lad with a laughable penis
Told a girl with a figure like Venus:
"We've got the whole night:
Do you think that we might
Let a small thing like this come between us?"

A lad who had gone round the bend
Spent ages impressing a friend.
He'd spin on his prick
Until he felt sick.
It used to involve daze on end.

Merely Males

A well-hung young fellow from Ealing
Has never found sex too appealing.
    When he's prone in a role,
    His improbable pole
Keeps pinning him flat on the ceiling.

        Cold weather unfailingly knocks
        Man's confidence down to his socks.
            He silently sobs,
            With nipples like knobs
        And his cock quite concealed in his rocks.

Disinfectant would shoot from Fred's dink
In a way that would make the girls blink.
        One said, "Though it's crude
        To be scrude with Jeyes' Flude,
I smell like a very clean sink."

        Said an anxious young man in Torquay,
        "I always sit down for a pee.
            This should not perplex
            Anyone *re* my sex:
        It means there are no flies on me."

Said Jock, "As a cock, it's just fine:
As hard as a rock, and it's mine.
        But it glows on erection -
        A torch-like projection,
Which means I get called Rise-and-Shine."

        Pete's perpendicular dick
        Is a pretty particular prick.
            With its tilt at the tip,
            It can shoot from the hip:
        A vertical squirtical trick.

Merely Males

Fred grumbled, "My trouble, you see,
My cock catches fire when I pee.
      I have to take aim
      To put out the flame.
It's difficult, aiming at me."

      Said a wistful old man in Dunoon,
      "Though I don't like complaining too soon,
            There's little attraction
            In life when the action
      Depends on the juice of the prune."

There's a lad to whom life has allotted
Two balls which are square-ish and spotted.
      One of his tricks
      Is to roll double six,
Then spin on his prick and get knotted.

      A lad with a lusty *libido*
      Had a tool like a trusty torpedo.
            Refreshingly rare,
            He'd aspired to a spare,
      As a possible pussy placebo.

Birthday suits give a chance of comparing
Accessories fellows are wearing.
      Their scrotums (or scrota) -
      One per cock is the quota -
Carry weight as a form of ball bearing.

      A foolish young fellow from Bude,
      Who stood on his head in the nude,
            Gave his eye such a bang
            With his over-long whang,
      It's a practice he's long since eschewed.

Merely Males

. . . he singes his jeans

Merely Males

Unthanked, Mother Nature imparts
To men's lives fairly startling starts.
Ungrateful new human
Is bathed by a woman,
Who goes on to powder his parts.

BORED STIFF

Though his willy was widely admired,
It wouldn't enlarge when required.
Then one day it dawned
That it did when he yawned,
Since when, he's enjoyed being tired.

But then, with a trollop named Sue,
When a yawn was a bit overdue,
He yawned broadly, and she
Said, "Your thing's boring me,
But I don't think I'm meant to bore you."

He yawned and replied with a grin,
"Let me explain: to begin,
I'm not bored: it's about
Not being tired out -
Much more about being tired in."

A randy young fellow called Sean
Stopped humping from dusk through to dean.
It's not that his dick
Is losing its kick,
It's just that his elbows are wean.

A fellow whose cock catches fire
Whenever he burns with desire,
Has found that this means
He singes his jeans
While watching the Luton Girls' Choir.

Merely Males

Said the doctor, "I trust you won't mope:
You're impotent, so you must cope
        With loss of espousal
        Of randy arousal.
There'll be no hard feelings, I hope."

Said an anxious young man from Belize,
"I'm afraid of the farting of fleas.
        Each eruption I hear
        Just increases my fear
That they'll bite while they're taking their ease."

        Said a man with two willies and stubble,
        "My bristles don't cause any trouble.
                If I'm shaving a few
                When she shouts for a screw,
        She knows that I'll come at the double."

"When I pee", Fred declared, "I discern
An occasional feeling of burn."
        And then he let slip
        He had terminal drip.
"So it's fatal?" Sue said, in concern.

        A man with the smallest of ends
        Was insistent on making amends,
                So he jiggled a lot
                With what he had got
        And sometimes he satisfied friends.

Fred went to a disco and said,
"Here's the viewpoint to which I am led:
        Had man been begat
        To look a right prat,
His willy would be on his head."

Merely Males

Said Fred, "I do not think it wise,
With a dick that is only half size,
    To bend it or fold it,
    So fannies can hold it -
Then shoot at the whites of my thighs."

The bulge in the front of Fred's thighs is
Just one of life's little surprises.
    It's not, to be fair,
    That his balls look so square:
It's just that they're four different sizes.

A lad with a prehensile poker
Plagued a lady by playing the joker.
    Because of its size,
    It slid through her thighs
And straight up her sternum to choke her.

Fred's balls tend to bump with a clang
Whenever he's having a bang.
    He explained this to Kay
    Just before their first lay,
But he said that she'd soon get the hang.

A despairing young man from Dundee
Whose dink is as short as can be,
    Says the jot that he's got
    Has got tied in a knot,
And he can't get his rocks off or pee.

Cries Paddy, with something that juts
From his jeans, and whose fly never shuts,
    "Oi've a steering wheel job
    On the end of me knob -
And it seems to be driving me nuts."

XXVI

SHALL WE JOIN THE LADIES?

A rather large lady, inclined
 To look for what fun she could find,
    Said, "Men like a game
    On my mountainous frame
While they squeeze my enormous behind."

            Genealogy fascinates some.
            Said Sharon, "I do think it's rum:
                Were it not for a fanny
                Belonging to Granny,
            I'd never have come from Mum's tum."

"For life to go on", murmurs Annie,
Grandpa must stick it up Granny,
        Making Father or Mother,
        Whose bit of the other
In time makes a prick or a fanny."

            Said a porky young lady, "I sweat.
            It rolls off in gallons, and yet
                My dad thinks it's ripping:
                He sells it as dripping.
            The locals take all they can get."

Sharon gives sex a new angle.
Her clitoris works like a mangle.
        A lad who intruded
        Was swiftly extruded
With something quite flattened to dangle.

Shall We Join the Ladies?

Tales of a teaser in Troon
With a 48 bust make men swoon.
What they don't realise is
God gave her two sizes -
A bell-push beside a balloon.

A well-endowed lady from Gwent
Took her bra off to sunbathe in Kent.
The locals agreed,
When they saw what she'd freed,
That topless is just what she ain't.

A beautiful babe called Chantelle
Cried, "I've just grown a penis! Oh, hell!"
One of her testes,
By common request, is
Now known as the ball of the belle.

Said a maid with a mountainous chest,
"I'll tell you what fellows love best.
After romping with me,
They can climb it to see
The sun as it sinks in the west."

They're monsters that make people stare:
They bounce when she jumps in the air.
It's not that they prove
The way mammaries move,
It's having two round and one square.

A young lady cried, "I'm bereft!
I'd sand and cement in my cleft -
And when I passed water,
It turned into mortar.
Since shitting a brick, I've none left."

Shall We Join the Ladies?

With a howl of dismay, Charlie's daughter
Cried, "Dad, I've a cleft full of mortar!"
        Said her dad, "Well, you went
        In that sand and cement
In your nothings before passing water."

        Said a flat-chested lady from Stroud,
        "I've not been unduly endowed,
                But I do not despair:
                I am also aware
        Of shoulder blades doing me proud."

Bewildered psychiatrists speak
Of a bored high-class lass as a freak.
        Whatever the knob,
        She will sleep on the job,
And her snorgasm's filed as unique.

        Said a middle-aged mermaid, on waking,
        "I hope that you don't think I'm faking:
                It really is strange,
                Now I've gone through the change,
        To find that my feet are both aching."

A flat-chested lass from Valletta,
Who'd never looked good in a sweater,
        Has now found the knack,
        With her bra on her back,
Of making her clothes fit much better.

        Said Susie, "I've never denied
        That my breasts are quite frequently eyed.
                But I don't think their size is
                The cause of surprises:
        It's having all four side-by-side."

Shall We Join the Ladies?

Said a lady who sat on a flute,
"At last I've the means to refute
    The unkindly aspersions
    Of those whose assertions
Imply that I don't give a hoot."

    A sassy young lassie named Jacquelyn
    Was classed as a crass piece of cracquelyn.
        Her slot was so slight
        That, try as they might,
    The lads couldn't quite get their tacquelyn.

There's a lass who goes dancing in Fife,
Whose bazookas break loose and cause strife.
    In sambas and congas,
    Her massive gazongas
Pack a punch that can threaten your life.

    A well-built young lady called Kay
    Had assets which led men astray,
        But according to rumours,
        Her famous bozoomers
    Would frequently get in the way.

A thoughtful young thing in Dundee
Ensures that refreshments come free.
    Drinks are drawn as desired
    From her tits 'til she's tired:
One's coffee, one's cocoa, one's tea.

    Said a satisfied lass, with a wink,
    "My lad's got the dinkiest dink.
        But that cute little cock
        Is as hard as a rock,
    And when it has shot it won't shrink."

XXVII
THE MEDIA

SAID a marketing girl, name of Nelly,
"Let's launch this new car with some welly!
Information, my ass!
Let's find something crass
To put in an ad on the telly."

Pat on Back for Eighth Army - a brief
Headline which caused undue grief,
   Making other troops wish a
   Great girl like Patricia
Would lie down to bring them relief.

If you fart on TV, you can tell,
When they say the next day it went well,
   That they thought you looked blooming,
   Or quite liked your grooming,
And never suspected your smell.

Special agent Dick Barton* could send
His listeners bemused round the bend.
   To the ladies' delight,
   They got Dick every night,
And four times as long each weekend.

* Dick Barton and the faithful Snowy had 15-
minute wireless adventures on week nights
and a one-hour omnibus repeat on Saturdays
during the 1940s.

The Media

Wind-breaking acts, it's admitted,
Fall down on TV when permitted.
An artiste said it showed her
In too good an odour -
Her pong, although strong, untransmitted

***

XXVIII
THERE WAS A...

There was a - *the usual way*
Of launching a limerick lay -
    Can never ring true,
    Alas, because who
Stresses was *when he speaks day-to-day?*

There was a's *the limerick text*
Whose absence might leave folk perplexed.
    And so, for tradition,
    You'll find this rendition
In this chapter and in the next.

*

THERE was a bullfighter from Spain
Whose lady had cause to complain.
    For foreplay, he'd lead her
    Just like the *corrida* -
All cloak and dagger and pain.

There was a young fellow called Bright,
Who never got form-filling right.
    When the question was *"Sex"*
    Without further checks,
He wrote down, *"On Saturday night."*

There Was A...

There was a young fellow called Jock,
Who answered graffiti in stock
    ("I'm nine inches by two:
    Am I O.K. by you?")
With, "Wonderful! How big's your cock?"

    There was a young fellow called Paul,
    With a ring through his thing and one ball.
        His girl friend, the shrew,
        At the end of a screw,
    Hung him up on a hook in the hall.

There was a young lass from Iraq
Who believed the manure from her crack
    To be fine for the vines
    She refined into wines
Whose bouquet, so they say, knocked you back.

    There was a young fellow from Bude
    Who said, "Kindly cease to allude
        To the fact that I pee
        While having my tea:
    It's all this convenience food."

There was a young lady who said,
"I am moral and very well bred.
    He was waving his ding,
    But it meant not a thing
Until we'd both climbed into bed."

    There was a young lady whose cleft
    Cried, "I'm in such a mess and bereft!
        Someone called Dick
        Popped in and was sick.
    I'm ever so glad that he left."

There Was A...

There was a young miss from Torbay,
With an ear, I am sorry to say,
    Each side of her cleft -
    Which regrettably left
Her lifting one leg, saying, "Eh?"

TWO OF A KIND

There was a young lady named Viv
With a clitoris built like a sieve -
    A pain in the main,
    And a strain for her swain,
Who declared, "She won't love and let live."

There was a young lady named Viv
With a clitoris built like a sieve -
    A lethal collusion
    Of lure and extrusion
Which shredded what lads had to give.

There was a young thing from St Mawes,
Whose cleft was a man-trap because
    It wasn't just sticky
    And clung to your dicky -
It bristled with teeth at its jaws.

There was a young lady who knew
The joys that the boys had in view.
    She said, "It's improper",
    And thus put a stopper
On what they'd intended to do.

There was an old man in a tree,
Who called from the top, "Eighty-three
    Years ago, like a mutt,
    I sat on a nut -
And now I am wanting a pee."

There Was A...

There was a young woman from Diss,
Who said, "Though I do it like this,
    I've heard in Rabat
    That they do it like that:
This and that make the other such bliss."

    There was a scoutmaster named Nick,
    Who had an incendiary dick.
        If he went off to camp
        When the weather was damp,
    It could kindle a fire pretty quick.

There was a young lady named Jacquelyn,
Who was famed as a fair bit of cracquelyn.
    But her cleft was designed
    In a manner confined,
And the chaps couldn't quite get their tacquelyn.

    There was a young man from Clovelly,
    Who farted while watching the telly.
        But he made not a sound,
        So the word got around
    He preferred being sneaky and smelly.

There was a young fellow from Purley,
Who never fulfilled any girlie.
    His minimal dick
    Used to come so damn' quick,
It was always too little, too early.

    There was a young man of Qatar,
    Who said, "It is better by far,
        This thing that I do,
        When I do it with you,
    Than it is when I do it with Ma."

There Was A...

There was a young fellow too smart
To be trapped by affairs of the heart.
      When safely in bed,
      He cautiously said,
"I am yours until dawn us do part."

      There was a young lass of Devizes
      Whose tits were of quite different sizes.
            The one on the right
            Was an eye-catching sight.
      The other three held no surprises.

There was a young lady from Woking
Who said, when she'd had a good poking,
      "I thought it was odd
      When they called him a god,
But, take it from me, they weren't joking."

      There was a young lady called Jude
      Who liked to be crude in the nude,
            With gestures so graphic
            She held up the traffic
      All the way from Clovelly to Bude.

There was a young fellow called Mark
Whose todger, while game for a lark,
      Was somewhat minute
      And, although rather cute,
Was tricky to find in the dark.

      There was an ex-convict, Adair,
      Whose wife was too ugly to bear.
            The lag had to shag
            With his head in a bag,
      Lest the one he put hers in should tear.

XXIX
A
PERSON
FROM BRUM

There was a young person from Brum,
Who was badly aware of his bum.
He said, "It's a farce:
Poets write of my arse,
Just because of the place whence I come."

His complaint is quite likely to pain us:
The practice, we'd say, is quite heinous.
But he'd find it the same -
Perhaps worse - if he came
All the way from the planet Uranus.

*

THERE was a young person from Brum,
Who was cross, constipated and glum.
He said craps in the closet res-
ult from suppositories.
That's a fact - and a pain in the bum.

There was a young person from Brum,
Whose standards would strike people dumb.
He said, "Folks may feel free
To write verse about me -
But not if they end it with *bum*."

A Person From Brum

There was a young person from Brum,
Who said, "Gender's confusing to some.
They write about me,
But they call me a he:
They've not noticed my tits or my bum."

There was a young person from Brum,
Who was joined to a twin at the bum.
Cans of beans caused a fart
Which blew them apart
In a diet devised by their mum.

There was a young person from Brum,
Whose whang would inhale but not come.
We cheered when he'd shown us
Our big breakfast bonus,
Whizzing round to collect every crumb.

There was a young person from Brum,
With a todger much longer than some.
"My banjo", he called it.
The girls were enthralled: it
Was always a pleasure to strum.

There was a young person from Brum,
Whose bathroom confused every chum
With its ultimate *coup,*
The vagina-like loo:
You'd just go to go, but you'd come.

✳ ✳ ✳

XXX
CORRESPONDENCE COURSE

DEAR Mummy, how can I begin
To tell you I'm living in sin
    With Cyril, who's naughty,
    Bald, fat and forty,
And constantly plies me with gin?

Dear Daughter, I don't give a damn:
You're really not fooling your Mam.
    So stop all this fuss:
    Just get on the bus
And tell me you failed your exam.

    A Parisian actor called Alec
    Wrote a postcard romantic and Gallic,
        But then went one better
        And sent a French letter -
    Quite equally Gallic, but phallic.

Possessive wife, mother of two,
Seeks ugly, withdrawn *au pair* who
    Won't take time off sick
    Or tease husband's prick,
Or spend too much time on the loo.

Forget the bad things you have feared:
I'm ugly - my friends call me weird.
    I'm fit as a flea,
    Last all day on one pee,
And come with my own prick and beard.

Correspondence Course

Dear Billy, Although I've no doubt
Of what contraception's about,
    I haven't the skill
    To be taking the Pill:
I've tried, but it kept falling out.

Dear Mary, I have to agree:
Contraception will not work for me.
    I bought from the pub a
    Device made of rubber -
But now I have found I can't pee.

    Dear Mum, Life at college is swell.
    I had a great night - you can tell,
        For, as a precursor,
        I buggered the bursar
    And then screwed his PA as well.

    Dear Son, It's a hoot, you'll agree:
    That the bursar should be HIV,
        Which he gave his PA
        In much the same way
    As, to start with, he got it from me.

Dear Trace, When we bonk, you will curse if I
Should explain that I can't; even worse if I
    Try to say that I'm gay
    While we have it away,
And for now have no plans to diversify.

Dear Steve, Can't believe that you're serious,
But further discussion would weary us.
    Forgive a cheap crack,
    But you get up my back -
And that could be quite deleterious.

XXXI

THE DEMON DRINK

For a code in the doze, he takes vodka.
  After dide, he seeks dew worlds to codka.
       It's always the sabe:
       He sees a dice dabe,
And whips out his willy to bodka.

       A theatregoer, while canned,
       Got confused in the loos at the Grand.
              He said, "Seats in the stalls
              Keep wetting my balls:
       I simply don't know where I stand."

"Jack", murmured Jill, "hasn't mastered
The evils of drink. He gets plastered.
              And as soon as he's pissed,
              He tries to insist
On his conjugal rights. He's a bastard."

       A perfect young gent, when in drink,
       Had manners which made people blink.
              As a matter of pride,
              He'd move plates aside
       Before peeing into the sink.

A lush of a lady called Queenie
Said, "Once I have had a martini,
              I am pleased to comply
              If a tool cares to try:
I'm not fussed about whopper or weeny."

The Demon Drink

Two glasses of brandy are handy
For making young Sandy feel randy.
    With a hand round each sphere,
    It is perfectly clear
That Sandy is thinking of Mandy.

      His problem will not be refuted.
      His words tend to come convoluted.
          The babbling bastard
          Is pie-eyed and plastered,
      Emotional, rat-arsed and newted.

A yeast-and-hops addict called Kay
Found her boobs filled with beer twice a day.
    Possibly pitiful,
    Sold by the titiful,
Ran out of glasses - Hooray!

      Fred said, "Go away, 'cos I'm busy."
      "But, Mommy", said Tommy, "why usy?"
          "I'm afraid", Mommy brayed,
          "When we've no lemonade,
      He pees in his beer, so it's fusy."

A lady who's living in sin
Attributes her downfall to gin.
    She proffered the slot
    That ladies have got,
And quick as a flash, he was in.

      Said a wine buff, "My piles are just fine
      For making a full-bodied wine.
          They hang from my rectum:
          Feel free to inspectum.
      Bottoms up! The bouquet is all mine."

The Demon Drink

. . . it's perfectly clear

The Demon Drink

. . . just now and again

The Demon Drink

A lady whose limit was two
Had one or two more than she knew.
        She woke up in bed
        With a fellow who said
He'd been thrilled with the things she would do.

        Said a frugal young lady from Maine,
        "I never bathe in champagne.
            I don't spend a nickel,
            But get the same tickle
        By farting just now and again."

XXXII

A CHANCE OF
A GHOST

THE ghost of a lusty old queen
Is still a keen screwing machine.
But though he's orgasmic,
He's just ectoplasmic,
And nobody knows where he's been.

The ghost of a randy old runt
Likes to goose pretty girls as a stunt.
If one starts to judder
Like a ship with no rudder,
You know he's just come round the front.

Fred once had a ghostly affair
With the Maid of Orleans - quite rare! -
He remarked, "It's a lark,
To be parking my arc
Somewhere moist where it's mostly fresh air."

An exorcist in from Kincaid
Found that folk were quite often dismayed.
He brought to his role
A prick like a pole,
With a cry, "There's a ghost to be laid!"

A ghostly philanderer called Sam
Continues to hump with his ham.
All his life, they would keep
Saying, "He's the black sheep."
He's now the invisible ram.

A Chance of a Ghost

The ghost of a long-dead old dean
Breaks wind just behind the rood screen.
    The choir is struck dumb:
    Not a soul sees him come -
But everyone knows when he's been.

    An elderly widow in Kerry
    Exclaimed, while she spilled all her sherry,
        'mid gasps, exhalations
        And pelvic vibrations,
    "My husband's come back for my cherry!"

The ghost of a young country maid
Was ever so glad that she'd strayed.
    She got back to base
    With a grin on her face
And the story of how she'd been laid.

    Said a masochist psychic, "My rule is,
    'Keep calm, keep alert and keep cool'." Is
        It true that his boast is,
        When grabbed by the ghosties,
    He asks to be grabbed by the ghoulies?

Some ghostly and randy hillbillies
Had naughty designs on young fillies.
    Ectoplasmic meanderings
    Fulfilled their philanderings:
While haunting, they gave them the willies.

    In a haunted old house on the coast,
    With his willy as stiff as a post,
        Was a bare-bottomed lad
        Doing press-ups like mad.
    He explained he was laying a ghost.

A Chance of a Ghost

At Graceland,* a groupie's one sentence
Showed shock, pleasure, truth and dependence.
  She pulsed and gyrated,
   Then gasped as she stated,
"The King is just making his entrance!"

   * Home of the late Elvis Presley and Mecca for
   devastated devotees.

  A lecherous poltergeist hid,
  'til kiss-and-tell lifted the lid,
    That he'd be in the groove,
    But the earth wouldn't move -
  Though damn' nearly everything did.

     ✳✳✳

XXXIII

OCCUPATIONAL HAZARDS

EXPERIENCE always imparts
That life as a rule's fits and starts.
But a stripper's baked beans
Are something that means
Her art's fits and starts, tits and farts.

An expert on shit in Penang
Said, "Craps that are quiet seem to hang
On a law which appends
To turds pointed ends,
So bums never close with a bang."

A footman said, "Nothing compares
To life with the girls below stairs.
A man's got to do
What a man's got to do.
The rhyme may be crap, but who cares?"

An accountant's wife blushed to find fame
For the number of twins to her name.
When she'd had her tenth pair,
She sighed in despair,
"Double entry's the name of his game."

A well-stacked young dancer named Joan
Has many routines which have shown
There's no way to freeze
36-double-Ds
Enjoying a life of their own.

Occupational Hazards

A model with assets to treasure
Compounded her personal pleasure
    In de-wrinkled eyes
    And liposucked thighs
With a bust she enhanced for good measure.

    A keeper of bees came to grief
    With a sting that was awkward, though brief.
        He got over the shock
        When he found that his cock
    Was a plonker that beggared belief.

A high-wire walker knows dire
Results come from slips: there transpire
    Testicular trauma,
    Pop-eyed performer,
And a voice which is higher than wire.

    A ball-juggling genius has shown
    The way that his prowess has grown.
        He's become quite a menace:
        Five golf balls, four tennis,
    Three cricket and two of his own.

An end-of-the-world man from Smite
Was preaching his message one night,
    When they said to him, "Son,
    Your flies are undone:
The end is already in sight."

    There once was a South Bengal lancer
    Who wanted to ring up a dancer.
        "Wrong number, old chap."
        "Don't give me that crap:
    If it is, why the hell did you answer?"

Occupational Hazards

A stripper's act got out of hand
With a peek whose appeal was unplanned.
    'twas not in her script,
    But she slipped as she stripped -
Bemusing the boys in the band.

    A stylish young lady named Heather
    Cut a dash with *panache* in tight leather.
        She worked at the Met
        And her get-up would get
    The forecasters wondering whether.

Said an old window cleaner one day
To a damsel, as starkers she lay
    On a rug of fake fur,
    "Excuse me, please, sir,
Am I right for the YMCA?"

    A fencing contractor did well
    To employ a young beauty named Nell.
        She helped with his filing
        And contract compiling
    And sometimes erections as well.

A postman who screws in full livery
Explains that to shaft makes him shivery.
    Girls gasp for *encores*,
    Then there's muted applause
When he says there's no second delivery.

    Conservationist Samuel, a builder,
    Spread his gospel each time that he thrilled a
        Young girl in bed
        And boastfully said,
    "That's what I'm saving for Hilda."

Occupational Hazards

A knight, while crusading in Palma,
Laid a lady who'd thought him a charmer.
    The damsel, though crushed,
    Chastely blushed at what gushed
From his dink through a chink in his armour.

    Said a builder, while working in Chard,
    "Making love's like cementing the yard:
        Can't do it all day,
        And it's not a good lay
    If you go on before it gets hard."

A sailor from South Tyne and Wear
Had a cock growing out of each ear.
    He now gives tuition
    In three-way coition.
It's fine if you don't call him queer.

    A bulldozer driver called Jim
    Invaded a young lady's quim.
        He said, when asked why,
        "I always keep my
    Earth-moving equipment in trim."

There's a secretary bird whom they're branding
A bit of a tease at Knots Landing.
    She swiftly arouses
    Man out of his trouses,
Then steals them and leaves the prick standing.

    Said a Ford Transit driver named Dan
    To a lass who loomed large in his plan:
        "The Eagle and Trumpet
        Will do for some crumpet."
    But she told him she'd have *coq au vin*.

Occupational Hazards

A sex-mad soprano in Devon
Makes love to a Welshman at seven,
    8.30 and 10.
    The neighbours know when:
She always sings *Penis from Evan.*

    An impotent milkman from Cheam
    Was dismayed when he ran out of steam -
        But taking Viagra*,
        Now shoots like Niagara:
    Two rocks and a hard place, full cream.

> * The male "wonder-drug" came to Britain in 1998.

Desmond Tinnie, a sculptor in Epsom,
Makes statues and tastefully drepsom.
    It's the size of their ends
    That fascinates friends,
And the way in which Des Tinnie shepsom.

A ROGUE-RHYTHM LIMERICK
. . . bound to offend the purists, but irresistible as a means
of recording a favourite joke.

Her laden butler shocked the Lady Sybil
In her bathroom, but she knew she shouldn't
                        quibble.
    In her bath, m'lady farted -
    But the message she'd imparted
Was, *"What about a water bottle, Wibble?"*

    Santa's been heard to complain
    Of Rudolph the reindeer again.
        "He breaks wind quite well,
        His nose runs like hell:
    This rain-nosed and rude deer's a pain."

Occupational Hazards

The Captain, RN, quite a demon,
Worked up a full head of steam an'
    Donated his sperm
    With credentials quite firm:
Officer, gent, able semen.

    Male strippers are left in a daze
    By the girls and the grans of Pipe Hayes.
        When they finish their act,
        They find for a fact
    That hoopla's the neighbourhood craze.

The photographer's model unzipped
Spectacular tits as she stripped.
    She wrecked his composure
    With double exposure.
His dong grew so long that he tripped.

    Said a lady who sought to divorce
    The back legs of a pantomime horse,
        "The neighbours all talk
        When we go for a walk -
    With his head up my jaxi, of course."

A music hall man said, "They cheer,
When I fart through my cock, loud and clear -
    Then quick as a wink,
    With a dip of my dink,
I put a new head on their beer."

    An expert on trees from Verdun
    Liked to guess people's ages for fun.
        In the nature of things,
        He counted their rings,
    And thought everybody was one.

XXXIV
FIRST IMPRESSIONS

A lovely young Swedish *au pair*
Achieved introductions with flair:
"Hello! I am Nordic!
I simply adordic!
How do you do! Put it there!"

Said Fred, "I've no wish to intrude.
I do hope you won't think me rude.
But I'll give you one quick
With a slippery dick -
And then you can finish your food."

A forthright young fellow in Dorking
Saw a charming young stranger out walking.
He said, "How do you do?
By the way, do you screw?"
She gasped, "Has some bleeder been talking?"

Good morning, I'm Fred: who are you?
I thought I'd say how do you do?
Talking of which,
You're a good-looking bitch,
So what is the chance of a screw?

Said a blushing young man from Devizes,
"My wedding night tackle comprises
An over-long dick:
When I chat up a chick,
It keeps on producing surprises."

First Impressions

A fellow called Cook got quite used
To pointing out when introduced
    To girls, that they'd find,
    If they pinched his behind,
They could say that their Cook had been goosed.

    "Hello! You're a nympho, they claim",
    Said Fred. "You're a good-looking dame.
        They tell me you choose
        Only cowboys or Jews.
    Hopalong Goldberg's the name. . ."

A lady who lounged in the nude
Said, "It's just that I like to exude
    My joy in my figure.
    I know dicks get bigger -
But I rarely do anything rude."

    Solemnity was the main feature
    Of the school's new geography teacher,
        But under the gravity,
        Sexual depravity
    Ensured quite a sociable feature.

A really quite rude Grenadier,
With an eye by his cock, and an ear,
    Was ever so dashing
    When going out flashing
And giving a shout of *"See hear!"*

    A plonker-proud fellow told Sue,
    "Your bell-push at waist height is new.
        I just came along,
        Pressed your ding with my dong,
    And delighted some bystanders, too."

XXXV

LOVE'S LABOUR'S LOST

TWO fatties felt Nature was mocking
Their efforts to start interlocking.
    Their overhung parts
    Defied all their arts
And stopped them well short of a docking.

    Her lover was always demonic,
    But now she has made things platonic.
        She says, "Sex is binned!
        It's gone with the wind!
    If we start, he just farts something chronic."

A bulbous young man said, "My failure
To stick out my dick and impailure
    Is largely because
    My stomach and yause
Don't help us to join·genitailure."

    An amorous fellow from Crewe
    Tries to prove for himself that it's true,
        When he blows in girls' ears,
        They'll respond to his leers.
    It's not, but he's deafened a few.

A mountainous couple, though pally,
Could not have a sexual rally.
    Their twin-peaks arrangement
    Of navel engagement
Precluded a prod in the valley.

Love's Labour's Lost

A corpulent couple of Brits
Blew hard as he dangled his bits.
    They see-sawed all day
    In an unfulfilled way,
Then he slipped and was gripped in her tits.

    A corpulent couple of Brits
    Made a mess of enmeshing their bits.
        As he perched, mound-on-mound,
        They rapidly found
    He would slide and be belly-on-tits.

The missionary cried, *"Hallelujah!*
From almost the moment I knujah,
    I feared that a man
    With my *enbonpoint*
Would never be able to scrujah."

    She said that his willy was vast,
    But its moment was always soon past.
        His 12-inch-long prick
        Always came very quick.
    As a rule, it was both hard and fast.

The mountainous maestro said sport
With voluptuous divae was fraught.
    "We bounce waist-to-waist,
    But we stay fairly chaste.
My baton, though upbeat, falls short."

    Said Fred, "I'd find sex more appealing
    If you managed to moan with some feeling."
        Next time he was grafting
        Away at his shafting,
    She said, "You've not painted the ceiling."

Love's Labour's Lost

Said Sharon, "Although your intention
Was something no lady should mention,
You're so bulky, my breach
Stayed just out of reach -
Which gave things an added dimension."

THE ICE MAN COMETH

An impotent toy-boy from Dover,
Who thought that his love life was over,
Now freezes his cock
As hard as a rock
And comes as The Cold Casanova.

Time after time, he's awoken
High hopes with his rigid love token.
He melts ladies' hearts,
But they then melt his parts
And find that his waters have broken.

Although Fred called Fifi *très bonne,*
He had a bad time getting on.
In the end, to excite him,
She started to bite him.
He came the day after she'd gone.

Said Jane, on the phone to a chum
Who'd remarked that she sounded quite glum,
"The trouble is Fred.
You should see him in bed:
He's lost all his get-up-and-come."

Seeking thrust for his marital art,
Fred fastened a squib to his part.
Poor bugger, instead,
Simply bounced round the bed,
While Sharon said, "Coo! What a fart!"

Love's Labour's Lost

A corpulent couple found lust
Made a fine sense of balance a must.
  Belly-to-belly,
  He'd cry out, "Oh, Nelly!"
And see-saw between every thrust.

  A randy young fellow from Kent
  Uncovered his carnal intent.
    She swiftly succumbed
    But was largely unplumbed,
  And she laughed at his natural bent.

A randy gargantuan Greek
Failed to screw more than two in a week.
  On his navel he'd rock,
  While his vertical cock
Dangled down, playing seeking the creek.

  Said a lad who had lost his *élan,*
  "Though two busty blondes were my plan,
    A *ménage à trois*
    Does *je ne sais quoi*
  To a fine and upstanding young man."

Said a highly frustrated young gent,
"They lowered the age of consent,
  But I waited so long
  To dib with my dong,
My pent-up intent simply went."

  A quick one-night stand can be hell.
  That was what drove Jack back in his shell.
    "It's a bind", he opined,
    "When you find a good grind,
  If her husband wants his turn as well."

Love's Labour's Lost

No lady would call Fred a liar
If he said that he burned with desire.
    She would just keep a watch
    On the state of his crotch,
And see that his cock was on fire.

    On the hearthrug in front of the Baxi,
    With a filly he'd lured with a fax, he
        Announced, "While I maul you,
        Let me think what to call you."
    She replied, "You can call me a taxi."

Said a pensive young thing in Valletta,
"Our love life perhaps might be better
    If we don't have it off
    Until after I doff
My bra, pants, jeans, thermals and sweater."

    Said Susie, "I cannot be thrilled
    By a penis whose contents are spilled,
        To leave it diminished
        Before I have finished,
    With lots of my lusts unfulfilled."

Said a lady, both wiser and older
Than the lad who had grabbed her and rolled her,
    "Let's delay these delights,
    And I'll take off my tights,
Then my feet might not fly past your shoulder."

    Said Jack, "Do you think we should sort of
    Seek the spice that our love life is short of?"
        Said Jill, "Good idea!
        From things that I hear,
    Foreplay is quite highly thought of."

Love's Labour's Lost

Said a large, almost globular man,
"Though I do try a screw when I can,
It's an unfulfilled lech,
As my plonker won't stretch
Quite as far as the old *enbonpoint*."

Sighed Jill, "Well, the doctor who's seen us
Told Jack, *'You've a very small penis.*
It's thin as a wafer
And clearly won't chafe her.'
That's why there's no feeling between us."

An eager young couple from Leek
Were united but right up the creek.
He'd not grabbed the Vaseline,
Putting his taseline,
But glue. They stayed close for a week.

An impotent *roué's* agenda
Included a weekend with Glenda.
His weak end was to prove
That the earth may not move
For a girl who's away on a bender.

A lively young lady named Jane
Cried, "Do it, then do it again!"
We're sad for poor Sid:
One do's all he did,
Then he said that he'd have to fetch Wayne.

I suggested a *ménage à trois*
With Fifi and Fred - but *ma fois!*
I have made a mistake:
The arrangements they make
Unfailingly don't include *moi*.

Love's Labour's Lost

A gut-bucket sighed, "Being round,
The job on the job I have found
  Is linking my dink
  With a fat lady's chink,
While we writhe, rock and roll, mound-to-mound."

  An anxious young man from Dundee
  Found after each love-making spree
    That his memory failed,
    And that's why he wailed,
  "Who are you and how was it for me?"

He says, "One, two, three!" and can score:
He gets an erection. What's more,
  Adding "Four!" , he will tame
  The brute. It's a shame
Girls ask, "What d'ya say One, two, three for?"

  A mini-dinked fellow called Trevor
  Was dismayed when his hardest endeavour
    Produced a wry smile,
    Then after a while,
  "Was that it? You don't say! Well, I never!"

He produced with a flourish and pride
His plonker, prepared for her ride.
  It had grown big and strong
  And ever so long,
But then it was sick and it died.

  A corpulent couple of Brits
  Made a mess of enmeshing their bits.
    As he rocked on her hillock,
    He felt quite a pillock,
  And scored far more misses than hits.

XXXVI

THE OLDEST PROFESSION

HOW puzzling Nature can be!
There's a back-to-front whore in Dundee,
Where men who lose heart
On this flat-chested tart
Find shoulder-blades size double-C.

Said Fifi, "With bondage, I've found
That punters will phone and come round,
To be trussed like a chicken
And whipped 'til they're kickin'."
Said the bishop, "That's fun, I'll be bound."

A back-to-front whore says that screwing
Is something she rather likes doing.
Her gentlemen find,
When they poke from behind,
She easily sees just what's brewing.

A call girl who called herself Venus
Said, "This is a secret between us:
I've developed the art
Of the rhythmical fart
To tickle a visiting penis."

An alien call girl from Zed,
Whose fanny went crosswise instead,
Explained to her friends,
"Men's other two ends
Hang over each side of the bed."

The Oldest Profession

A tart with her cleft in her head
Dismayed all her callers in bed.
  This obvious orifice,
  Unnerving to novices,
Had made her decide not to wed.

  A hardly-inhibited whore
  Had a cleft that was like a small door,
    Sexual voracity,
    Cubic capacity
  And clients who came four by four.

A whore in the desert admitted,
"A bonk's like a file being fitted -
  Uniting a stand
  That's covered in sand
With a cleft that's less envied than pitted."

  A helpful young hooker called Fay,
  Whose friction-free cleft caused dismay,
    Found sandpaper lining
    Proved much more confining,
  Though prone to wear foreskins away.

Said a tart who was trading as Annie,
"I am sure the success of my fanny
  Reflects Nature's plan
  To see that a man
Associates nookie with cranny.

  A freezing young tart, playing sentry
  Outside in the street, said, "The gentry
    Could give me more fun
    Than ever they've done
  Up front up to now up the entry."

The Oldest Profession

A sailor in search of some yo-ho
Found a tart with a heart down in Soho.
      But she cried, "Don't be daft!"
      And she laughed at his shaft.
So Soho yo-ho? Oh, no, ho-ho!

      There are girls for whom love is retailable,
      And those who are just not assailable,
            And those who are known,
            Either supine or prone,
      To be usually freely available.

An impotent lad found his flame
When he entered a house of ill-fame.
      Phenomenal filly
      Worked well on his willy.
He's ever so glad that he came.

      A frisky young fellow called Price,
      Whose genitals worked like a vice,
            Got a call girl called Jean
            With her chin caught between
      Two rocks and a hard place - how nice!

A call girl who always looked smart
Had a failing which set her apart.
      Every night, as she sinned,
      She always broke wind:
They called her the tart with a fart.

      A lady accustomed to cocks
      Customighty big swear word at Jock's.
            After lying in wait
            With herself as the bait,
      Courtesan courteseye courtespox.

The Oldest Profession

Fred was found in a brothel, which left
Our hero but briefly bereft.
"As I'm in a cleft stick",
He said, dipping his dick,
"I shall stick where I am, in a cleft."

Said a raddled old tart, "I protest.
Screw-now-and-pay-later's a pest.
If payment's delayed,
It will ruin the trade.
Up front is the way things work best."

A plantsman got up people's noses
With practical jokes and daft poses.
He frightened a tart
As she practised her art,
When he said it was coming up roses.

A raddled old tart said, "I find
A holiday's good for my mind -
Refreshing the me
That the clients don't see,
Before I get back to the grind."

For a lovely young call girl called Kay,
Protected sex seems here to stay.
At the foot of the bed,
Her rottweiler, Ted,
Stands guard while she has it away.

A call girl who tried Tal-y-llyn
Got clients steamed up with a grin.
They went up by rail
For cash on the nail -
In a tin labelled *Wages of Sin.*

The Oldest Profession

The hard-up young call girl was brash,
Explaining her marks with *panache.*
    She said to her mum,
    "I get thrashed on my bum,
'cos that's what I am - strapped for cash."

    A feminist tart of great flair
    Had a system surprising and rare.
        Though meekly compliant
        With the needs of a client,
    She insisted on paying her share.

It's no shock that a call girl named Alice's
Views prove so wrong on analysis.
    There's not much relief
    From mistaken belief
In a life that is chock full of phalluses.

    A whorehouse allotment caused doubts
    In patrons pulled in there by touts
        When they saw, they allege,
        Their meat and two veg
    Topped up with some fine brothel sprouts.

A tart in Boulogne, name of Fleur,
When a matelot was visiting her,
    Wouldn't let him be late
    If his ship sailed at eight,
But cried aloud, *"À l'eau! C'est l'heure!"*

    A hooker who's also a cook
    Tried writing a prize-winning book.
        Said the cook who's a hooker,
        "I'll make my book Booker,
    If each judge, for an hour, books my nook."

The Oldest Profession

A lascivious lady for whom
Men queued to be rude in her room
        Said, "A fellow called Bob,
        Who died on the job,
Was blaming the old crack of doom."

A punter felt rather a prat
When his tadger was trapped and pressed flat.
        His ardour was damped
        When he found he was clamped
By a vice girl who really was that.

        Said a floozie called Susie, "I've faced
        All kinds of scrotes I've embraced,
                But they're out on their necks
                If they want oral sex.
        I suppose it's a matter of taste."

Said a raddled old tart, "Nothing rocks
My confidence more than the knocks
        From those who besmirch
        My years of research
In search of identical cocks."

        "Well, well!" said the vice girl. "That's nice!
        Your willy is wedged 'twixt my thighce!
                Chaps never suspect,
                When they're getting erect,
        That they'll find where I've hidden my vice."

When asked, "Do you smoke while you screw?",
A call girl said, "Maybe I do,
        If ever constriction
        Creates enough friction -
Though I'm not in the best place to view."

The Oldest Profession

When a punter had died on the job,
The tart with a heart said, "Poor Bob!
     Though his ticker was dicky,
     I gave him a quickie,
And then we had one for his nob."

          Said the tart, "From the start, to be blunt,
          I thought the runt's stunt an affront.
               He asked me for credit!
               As soon as he said it,
          I told him I liked it up front."

Two call girls at lunch, to unwind:
One said, "I must dash! Do you mind?
     But I know if I'm late
     That the punter won't wait.
It's a bugger - but back to the grind."

          There's a tart with a heart who won't trust
          The wimps who just lust for her bust.
               If one lays his fingers
               On one of her swingers,
          She tells him she's thirsting for thrust.

Wee Jean of the generous orifice
Tends to take it to treat local offices.
     She times her arrival
     So someone's hard drive'll
Download where the corner for coffees is.

          An impotent lad got to spend a
          Weekend with a floozie called Brenda,
               And after the act,
               She remarked with great tact,
          "It's a change to get off on a bender."

The Oldest Profession

Said a floozie called Susie, "Although
You have heard I'm a bird who will show
    A slick mix of tricks
    With up to six dicks,
It ain't necessarily so."

    A diffident fellow called Pat
    Made a tryst with a tart in a flat
        But he muttered, "I know it'll
        End up all coital.
    No way I'm standing for that."

A whore in a harem in Suez
Can't usually choose who her scruez.
    If he's late, she's been known
    To proceed on her own.
When told she's a tart, she says, "Whuez?"

    A pools coupon madam and whores
    Like to give all their clients applause -
        One point, that's to say,
        When they have it away;
    Three each for a pair of score drawers.

A call girl who called herself Fran
Took her calling beyond the job plan,
    And she sometimes caused strife,
    Always calling the wife
To say, "I've just had your old man."

    No danger you might drop a clanger
    With a tart who works cars in Stavanger:
        Although she extols
        A roll in a Rolls,
    She still likes a bang in a banger.

XXXVII

A MESSAGE MISTAKEN

A curious curate from Bicester
Learned difficult words from a list. A-
las, this young parson
Mixed incest with arson
And swiftly set fire to his sister.

Said a carpenter, seeking some twine,
To his mate, who he thought would do fine,
"Got some string on yer, Dick?"
Said his mate, "Don't be sick!
That's none of your business - it's mine!"

Birth Announcements clerk brought Mum to tears,
Asking Dad, who had had a few beers:
"How many insertions?"
He, counting exertions,
Said, "Five times a week for four years."

A haulage contractor's wife, Nan,
Asked whether she liked *coq au vin,*
Replied, "I am sorry:
Events in the lorry
Concern only me and my man."

A vampire dressed as a toff
Chased two nuns with a sneer and a scoff.
Hissed one, at a loss,
"Quick! Show him your cross!"
Said the other, "I will! *Bugger off!"*

A Message Mistaken

. . . show him your cross

A Message Mistaken

"Make your bids", said the man with the mike.
"Sack o' cacky! Just start where you like!"
    That bag of manure
    Made £100 - sure!
Well, it *SOUNDS* like a Jap motor bike.

    A rather deaf farmer called Heep,
    Caught urgently shafting a sheep,
        Explained, "It's occurred
        Every night since I heard
    That he who mounts sheep gets to sleep."

Two gardeners, Plantem and Pickem,
Surprised a good lady in Wickham.
    They replied with a shout
    To her cry of, *"Prick out!"*
"They're out - tell us where we can stick 'em!"

    The ape hadn't mated in ages.
    Thinking Fred might oblige for the wages,
        They said, "Fred, there's a fee."
        Fred replied, "Fine by me!
    Do you mind if I pay it in stages?"

TWO OF A KIND

Jack pulled, with a finger and thumb,
Jill's frock from the crack in her bum.
    When she gave him a smack
    And a look that was black,
He poked it back whence it had come.

Behind a young lady, old Jack
Tugged her dress, which was stuck in her crack.
    He got thumped for his stunt,
    So, round at the front,
When he saw it hung loose, poked it back.

A Message Mistaken

When told that Fred's bathroom was pink,
A designer said, "What would you think
Of a *boudoir* the same?"
Fred said, "Great! What a shame
We all wash our bums in the sink."

She said, with a coy little grin,
"Bristol Cream is my naughtiest sin."
Said Fred, "That's all right.
A bit later tonight,
I'll help you with rubbing it in."

Jane knows intuition is right.
That's why she stripped off in delight,
To encourage a guy
Who was painfully shy.
He was trying to ask for a light.

Two nuns, Sisters Mercy and Jo,
Topped their car up with fuel from a po,
As that's where they'd stored it.
One driver adored it.
He cried, "When you've faith, it should show!"

Said Fred, in the gents' for a pee,
"You've far more to piss with than me.
I've always been told
You've a four-finger hold."
Joe said, "Yes, but I'm pissing on three."

In new lodgings, a randy old queen,
On hearing that Billy (18)
Walked each morning at four,
Left open his door. . .
To the biggest alsatian he'd seen.

A Message Mistaken

"It's the blind man!" The call was a bind
For the nun in the bath: never mind!
    "You'd better come in!"
    So he did, with a grin:
"Great tits! What's your plan for the blind?"

    A former car driver named Russ
    Now travels to work on the bus.
        He prompted dismay
        With his pay and display.
    It was what he displayed caused the fuss.

Fred, dining in France, cried, "Great Scot!
There's a fly in my soup! *Une mouche* - hot!"
    "UN mouche", waiter said.
    "Good heavens!" said Fred,
"What wonderful eyesight you've got!"

    People know a young fellow called Nick
    Has a most individual trick.
        They're surprised when he shows
        What he does with his nose:
    They'd thought it would feature his dick.

"I've gone blind!" exclaimed old Mrs Brown,
When she stumbled while walking in town.
    "What fingers", asked Thrupp,
    "Am I putting up?"
". . . and paralysed from the waist down!"

    After crying, *"Free will is for all!"*
    The preacher had no chance at all
        Of saying *"Absurd!"*
        To the girls who had heard
    And who thought they'd be having a ball.

A Message Mistaken

. . . your plan for the blind?

A Message Mistaken

Said a lady who, feeling quite flirty,
Had got him to bed at 5.30,
    "Say *oil, grease* and *grime,*
    And *fat, mud* and *slime:*
I've heard that it's fun, talking dirty."

With his hands in his crotch, there was Jack.
She could see he had taken a whack.
    "Shall I rub it?" she said,
    So he lay on the bed
And she rubbed, but one thumb still went black.

Said a blonde, "I'm a lesbian who
Doesn't screw with a scrote such as you.
    For sex, I enjoy
    A girl, not a boy."
Fred said, "Gee! I'm a lesbian, too!"

Puffed Thor, "I'd have been quite a prat if I'd
Not screwed you like that until gratified.
    But there's just one thing more:
    I must tell you I'm Thor."
"Tho am I", breathed the lass, "but I'm thatithfied."

"To lose armpit hair", said Gervaise,
"Rub this cream on in three different ways."
    "You'll have to try harder:
    It's for my Chihuahua."
". . . and don't ride your bike for six days."

Said an elderly spinster called Mabel,
"Snooker sounds like a game I'm unable
    To watch, if it's true
    I'll see a long queue,
While they play with their balls on the table."

Said the Heir to the Throne, who was seen
In a hat of fox fur on the green,
  "I said to my mother,
  'I'm off to Cymstrotha'.
'Wear the fox hat', said the Queen."

XXXVIII

A VERY LONG THING

A man with a very long beast
Wouldn't mind, you would find, in the least,
    Were he laid by design
    In the depths of a mine,
With his whang up the shaft (when deceased).

    A man with a very long chopper
    Bunged it into his bum as a stopper.
        His secret sensation
        Is small consolation:
    He's buggered himself good and proper.

A man with a very long cock
Sent girls into tremor and shock.
    It twirled with the scope
    Of a Mid-Western rope
And lassoed the grandfather clock.

    A man with a very long dibber
    Said, "My wife used to think me a fibber.
        Then I showed her the snake
        And she started to quake,
    Gesticulate, panic and gibber."

A man with a very long dick
Said its name was too short and too slick.
    "As my whang's monumental,
    It's quite fundamental
To call it King Richard damn' quick."

A Very Long Thing

A man with a very long dickie
Found love-making awfully tricky.
       He sighed for a ride,
       But an hour for each slide
Sort of lessened his chance of a quickie.

       A man with a very long dink
       Vaulted home on it, quick as a wink.
           His means of propulsion
           Did not cause revulsion:
       He passed you before you could blink.

A man with a very long dink
Said, "It's bigger each day! Do you think
       That I ought to report
       To a quack of some sort?"
Said his friends, "That depends: try a shrink."

       A man with a very long dong
       Said, "A chick on my dick can't go wrong.
           When I've screwed her to hell,
           We don't say farewell:
       She leaves, sort of gasping, 'So long!'"

A man with a very long dong
Said, "I'm sure the design must be wrong.
       When it stands like a pole
       In a gratified hole,
I know that my knob's in Hong Kong."

       A man with a very long dong
       Said, "A bimbo showed things can go wrong,
           Causing pain in my willy
           As I camped at Caerphilly,
When she tripped on the tip in Hong Kong."

A Very Long Thing

A man with a very long end
Broke his leg and just loved to pretend
The calamitous cock
Tucked into his sock
Was the splint for his nurses to tend.

A man with a very long end
Said, "A bird has to learn to depend
On me for a screw
By going to Crewe
When we've just said goodbye in Southend."

A man with a very long friend
Said, "Girls like to watch it extend,
But they find it a trauma
To have to perform a
Turn when they've run to the end."

A man with a very long hampton
Had problems on mountains he campton.
Though all right at night,
By dawn's early light,
With campers about, it got stampton.

A man with a very long heinie
Sat down in Kent, facing the briny,
While it bored out the tunnel
Preparing the Chunnel
And popped up in France, red and shiny.

A man with a very long jack
Said, "I don't want to boast, but its knack,
As it's fairly gigantic
And spans the Atlantic,
Is to rub itself up coming back."

A Very Long Thing

A man with a very long jizzy
Lets it help out his wife when she's busy,
    But its rolling-pin role
    Makes him spin on his pole,
While his head bumps the floor 'til he's dizzy.

    A man with a very long jobby
    Says he calls on his friends as a hobby.
        His knob slides upstairs
        And delights the au pairs,
    While he rings the bell in the lobby.

A man with a very long member
Doesn't know about love's dying ember.
    His remarkable gear
    Earns praise all the year,
Though it's best between March and December.

    A man with a very long part
    Developed an untoward art.
        Self-buggery grew
        From the need to subdue
    An otherwise rip-roaring fart.

A man with a very long pecker
Said, "On buses, they call me a wrecker.
    I'm charged double fares
    When it trails down the stairs
On an otherwise staid double-decker."

    A man with a very long phallus
    Said people could sometimes be callous,
        But a kind-hearted pal
        Laid it right down the Mall
    And three times round Buckingham Palace.

A Very Long Thing

'... middle and leg

A Very Long Thing

A man with a very long peg
Played cricket, and umpires would beg
    Him not to amuse them,
    And worse still confuse them,
By asking for middle and leg.

    A man with a very long pleaser
    Can raise the thing up by degrees - a
        Fact he can stress
        With flair and *finesse*
    When he props up the Tower of Pisa.

A man with a very long plonker
Had a problem he never could conquer.
    When his wife went to bed,
    She left poor old Fred
Aiming blind in the kitchen to bonk her.

    A man with a very long pole
    Had a pretty good time on the whole.
        He screwed a young lass
        From her front to her ass,
    And when he was through, shouted, "Goal!"

A man with a very long pole
Had never discovered its role.
    Then he got to lie down
    With a lady from town,
And had a good time on the whole.

    A man with a very long prick
    Said, "I can't get it out very quick.
        I do it in stages:
        It seems to take ages -
    The far end is four inches thick."

A Very Long Thing

A man with a very long rivet
Said, "It needs all the space I can give it.
It hangs round the garden,
And if it should harden,
It tunnels out under the privet."

A man with a very long rod
Said girls sometimes thought it was odd
That now and again
He would clear out a drain
While asking what chance of a prod.

A man with a very long snake
Said, "Nature has made a mistake -
But I have to give praise
For the wonderful ways
It finds to keep ladies awake."

A man with a very long tadger
Found girls used to pester and badger.
When they shouted, *"Encore!"*
And cried out for more,
He would say, "Go away, I've just hadger."

A man with a very long thing
Is amazed at the joy it can bring.
When he plumbs a young lass
It comes out through her ass,
And her friend on the end starts to sing.

A man with a very long tiggy
Sat up with a lass and a ciggy.
She said, "One never mentions
Size, shape or dimensions -
But, bloody hell, that was a biggy!"

A Very Long Thing

A man with a very long tine
Says Germans have all found it fine.
    They offer protection
    To every erection,
Then use it for crossing the Rhine.

    A man with a very long todger
    Confided one day to his lodger,
        "The end's far from nigh,
        And that explains why
    It's birds out of sight that I roger."

A man with a very long tool
Tripped over the end like a fool;
    Got over the shock,
    Tucked it down in his sock,
And calls it a splint or a rule.

    A man with a very long tool
    Kept the tip in a classroom at school.
        He'd seek out the end
        On the bike of a friend,
    But the end stayed ahead as a rule.

A man with a very long tool
Said, "I once felt a bit of a fool.
    There was laughter in class
    When it tickled the ass
Of a girl in the front row at school."

    A man with a very long totem
    Said, "Girls walk its length, then devotem-
        selves to the job
        Of admiring my knob
    And my wrinkled retainer, old Scrotum."

A Very Long Thing

A man with a very long totem
Said, "My balls are to scale, if you note 'em.
    They bang as they hang,
    With a sonorous clang,
In one hell of a bell of a scrotum.

    A man with a very long weapon
    Said, "Sometimes, it's easy to step on,
        But its length is just right
        When it's rolled out at night
    For the upper-sixth girls to do prep on."

A man with a very long whang
Told a girl who had sighed for a bang:
    "A pleasure, my dear:
    I'll hang around here.
You'll find the far end in Penang."

    A man with a very long whang,
    Who knelt on his nuts as he sang,
        Went soprano from bass
        With a rather strained face
    And a lack-lustre cluster to hang.

A man with a very long whang
Said, "The birds on the end like the bang,
        Though they have to get back
        To take up the slack.
It's a rather slow screw from Penang."

    A man with a very long whang
    Said, "The ladies quite soon get the hang
        Of finding a screw
        In the sidings at Crewe
    Requires their desires in Penang."

A Very Long Thing

A man with a very long whang
Is admired from Penarth to Penang,
     But he's sick of his dick,
     Which is six inches thick,
As he's not got a slot for a bang.

     A man with a very long willy
     Said, "Each time I pee, I feel silly.
          There's no other man
          Dips his dick in the pan.
     It's not only wet, it's quite chilly."

A man with a very long willy
Drew a face on his knob with great skill: he
     Then gave not a damn:
     Took it walks in the pram,
Saying, "Who'll come and tickle young Billy?"

     A man with a very long willy
     Says when doves come to perch he feels silly.
          And he's grown to depend
          On the wheel at the end
     For pushing ahead where it's hilly.

A man with a very long wire
Likes to help the brigade at a fire.
     All that one knows is,
     They roll out their hoses
And his is the talk of the shire.

***

XXXIX

SLIGHTLY SAUCY

THE lecherous leanings of Jock
Were curbed by his dad round the clock.
 He put with great glee
 Something into Jock's tea -
As often as not, just Jock's cock.

 Suicidal signoras who seize a
 Chance on the Tower of Pisa,
  But choose the wrong side,
  Just have a long ride,
 Which scratcha da assa and knisa.

A lovely young girl at De Witts
Has a pair of quite memorable tits.
 Her guests all approve
 Of the way that they move
When she throws out their bread, nuts and bits.

 "Falling in love by design",
 Said a practical lady, "is fine.
  Whenever I fall",
  She added, with gall,
 "It's HIS length I measure, not mine."

A naturist lass from The Wyke
Lay down to get brown on a hike.
 A deckchair attendant
 Saw bottom resplendent
And used her for parking his bike.

Slightly Saucy

No man, so they say, is an island,
On lowland or wet land or dry land.
    Although he feels insular,
    Penile peninsula
Provides some relief and some high land.

    A well-endowed lady who's rudish
    Likes to go everywhere sort of nudish.
        She undertakes sorties,
        Displaying her naughties,
    And thrusts *têtes-à-têtes* on the prudish.

Young Sharon keeps causing hilarity:
Bares her breasts so you view them with clarity.
    This warm-hearted bint
    Charges twopence a squint -
Free of tax as she does it for charity.

    A plonker-proud fellow called Roy
    Gave himself a Welsh town to enjoy:
        One day while well randy,
        Tattooed *Tonypandy.* . .
    Which rapidly shortened to *Toy.*

The ageing of man, grumbles Wendy,
Makes it hard to describe him as trendy.
    His joints all go stiff,
    Which would not be bad if
What used to be stiff wasn't bendy.

    Fred left the pictures one night,
    With a hand that was swollen and white.
        It was nothing too drastic:
        The knicker elastic
    Had just been abnormally tight.

Slightly Saucy

Ignoring the clothes and the clamour is
A world full of males who think glamour is
    Not legs and not lips
    And not soft-curving hips,
But bloody great mountainous mammaries.

    To travel by post, for a jest,
    Make sure you're correctly addressed,
        Then go like a parcel,
        With stamps on your arcel
    And postcodes all over your chest.

There's hardly a fellow alive
Who won't start to perk up and thrive
    If a bint shows a bit
    Of a hint of a tit
With the smell of Chanel Number Five.

    In the street, a young fellow called Gus
    Told a girl, "I'm not making a fuss -
        But one tit's hanging out."
        She replied with a shout,
    "Oh, my Gawd! We've left Bab on the bus!"

Don't rhyme me with *moon, June* or *spoon!*
Don't call me a spermatozoon!
    I can't let this go on!
    I'm a spermatozoon -
Or else your next babe's a baboon.

    A randy Red Indian chief
    Is always in need of relief.
        The scope of the totem
        That goes with his scrotum
    Is something that beggars belief.

Slightly Saucy

Sextuplets born in Samoa:
A triumph for spermatozoa!
    Said the sperm who was dad,
    "I'm a bit of a lad.
What's more, I'm a hell of a goa."

    Babes? Sperm, if we really believe 'em,
    Go to work on an egg to conceive 'em.
      When a sperm takes a wife,
      It must be for life,
    And not entail ovum-and-leave 'em.

At home, or in far distant lands,
It's known that she sits and he stands
    To do what dogs found
    Needs a leg off the ground:
It's all such a bore, shaking hands.

    Girls with *panache* are the best.
    Their flair without fail has impressed.
      One called at the vicar's,
      Stripped down to her knickers,
    And said that she felt over-dressed.

Fred is a fellow who makes
Very few social mistakes -
    Though he did say to Sue,
    As he went to the loo,
He'd be back in a couple of shakes.

    Aged 80, Fred cried, "Life can fill me
    With pleasure and pride! It can thrill me!
      I'm jumping for joy!
      I've fathered a boy!
    If the missus discovers, she'll kill me!"

Slightly Saucy

An afternoon's furtive delights
Cause two of the world's strangest sights:
    A man in short socks
    Displaying his rocks,
And a girl squirming into her tights.

    A helpful young lass from Devizes
    Ensures life is full of surprises.
        She gives the lads shocks
        By stroking their cocks,
    Since that's how her pleasure arises.

A well-endowed gay says it's true
That problems and pleasures accrue.
    He gets a bit sick
    Of his columnar dick,
But does enjoy joining a queue.

    Cried a grateful young man from East Sheen,
    "How faithful my mother has been!
        I do think it's nice
        That she's strayed only twice -
    With the Met and the Wasps' third fifteen."

In ladies' and gents', we can see,
Inflation replaced £sd.
    We went for a penny
    In Abergavenny,
But now we can't go for a p.

    "Oh, heavens! I've stepped on your dong!"
    Cried a lady he'd not known for long.
        "Don't worry, my dear,
        I'll survive - never fear",
    Gasped Fred (who was sure he was wrong).

Slightly Saucy

Fred gave all his colleagues a start,
Disguised as his cock, with great art.
    To his boss, he said, "Nick,
    You called me a prick -
So here I am, looking the part."

    Six damsels, each draped in a duster,
    Are pretty well certain to fluster
        A lad with quick flicks
        Showing size 36
    In pairs or a frightening cluster.

Said a maiden from South Borehamwood,
"If you liked that the way that you should,
    I know Mum will be
    Really happy for me:
She's always said I should be good."

    There's an area hairy where girlier
    Girls make men straight in the curlier.
        Pointing out Andy,
        Who's upright and randy,
    Sue whispers, "It's one I made earlier."

Fred's dirty great grin takes some shifting
When he thinks secret thoughts and starts drifting.
    If you look at his jeans,
    You can see what he means
When he says they're not pure, just uplifting.

    The young lady gasped, "That's a whopper!"
    On first catching sight of Fred's chopper.
        Then she turned a bright red
        And jumped into bed,
    To help him do something improper.

Slightly Saucy

A well-hung young man from Carlisle
Had always a satisfied smile -
    A lecherous grin
    That hinted of sin,
And a reason that stuck out a mile.

    Survival of man, one suspects,
    Depends on survival of sex -
        Insistent insertions'
        Exploding exertions,
    Combining concave and convex.

A frantic young fellow from Dorset,
Whose girl had a willy-proof corset,
    Declared, "When I've tried
    To get it inside,
She's always said, 'Freddie, don't force it!'"

    He romped with Penelope, founding
    The censure that soon was rebounding.
        His joys - there were many -
        When in for his Penny,
    Have gone now he's in for a pounding.

The sport that absorbed Aberystwyth -
Uniting the organs it pystwyth -
    Alas, proved too fraught
    For willies too short
For girls to pursue or persystwyth.

    A gratified lady from Stoke
    Said, "Underground trains full of folk
        Are such a tight squeeze,
        I get poked as I please,
    By bloke after bloke after bloke."

Slightly Saucy

Said Fred, "Though I think she's *très bong*
In a swimsuit, it's surely quite wrong
    That a filly so fair
    With divine *derrière*,
Should be sliced up her slot by a thong."

    Prince Chas, with great brass, spoke of bed
    With an officer's wife and it led
        Himself and Camilla
        To be seen as samilla
    To Wallis and Great-Uncle Ted.

A woman soon grows to depend
On the tricks she has learned from a friend
    To strengthen her plan
    For getting a man.
They're all just a means to an end.

    There are many strange moments about:
    Everyone has them, no doubt.
        But few are as silly
        As hunting your willy
    When Y-fronts are on inside-out.

A busty colleen, without warning,
Cavorted as daylight was dawning,
    Unclothed on the lawn
    And was spotted by Sean,
Who commented, "Top of the morning."

    A furtive and brief stolen kiss
    Produces a moment of bliss
        Which can lead, so it's said,
        To a session in bed
    And a cry of, "Good heavens! What's *this?*"

Slightly Saucy

Cried a lass who would strip but not tease,
As she tore off her blouse, "Look at these!
    With one in each hand,
    A fellow can't stand
And is likely to sink to his knees."

    Said a groper who groped in Valletta,
    "I took off my gloves when I metta.
        She quite understands
        What this did for my hands:
    I told her I'd never felt betta."

Said Janet, "You cannot deny
Some fellows keep catching the eye.
    Have you noticed how Jock
    Is waving his cock
And asking who said he was shy?"

    Sobbed the duke, "I have had such a fright!
    My son has 'come out': is this right?
        Sudden conversion
        To animadversion!
    My heir has gone gay overnight!"

With agencies' learning the art
Of helping along Cupid's dart,
    Computerised dating
    Now speeds up the mating:
The love bytes are there from the start.

    A shapely young shopgirl called Jude
    Sold software while naughtily nude.
        Her floppies entranced
        The lads as she danced,
    And a nice little sideline ensued.

Slightly Saucy

Gratified ladies know when
Viagra's involved, because then. . .
Inspection, elation,
Erection, duration,
Longstanding upstanding. Amen.

There wath a young lath called Thamantha
Who fanthied herthelf ath a dantha.
She thlipped at a dithco,
Thome plathe in Linlithgow,
And the boyoth took turnth to romantha.

There's a pest for whom zest is expressed
In divesting two nests from her chest -
So she must trust your lust
With the thrust of her bust,
Though it's best if her chest can rest dressed.

Some happy old girls in the Gower
Have got a young stud in their power.
He's tied on the bed,
Stripped and stroked, which has led
To hoop-la for many an hour.

A lap-dancing club is a place
Where damsels who've spurned social grace
Will strip off their gear,
Stick a tit in your ear
And waggle their bum in your face.

A sex-starved young lady named Kay
In her diary wrote, "Got none today.
Nor today. Nor today.
Nor today. Nor today."
At which point, Kay threw it away.

Slightly Saucy

... on some rather long flights

Slightly Saucy

Two well-endowed pranksters on Sark
Had knob-ends which shone in the dark.
    From midnight to three,
    They would help ships at sea
On to rocks with their cocks, for a lark.

    Said a bimbo, while looking the part
    In moulded shorts (state of the art),
        When Fred cried, "Lord knows
        How you get into those":
    "Gin-and-tonics would be a good start."

An amateur stripper called Hannah
Used to take off her clothes for a tanner.
    Now it's $2^{1}/_{2}$p,
    But she's turned 83
And the flair's sort of gone from her manner.

    In a longest-cock contest at Clee,
    The open class helped us to see
        Six inches or seven,
        Though average for Devon,
    Will just raise a smile in Torquay.

Said a big-mouth who'd just had a date
With a glorious sex-bomb called Kate,
        "I'm a man who deserves
        What she serves with her curves -
And she knows, 'cos I gave it her straight."

    One of life's little delights
    Is to sleep in the nude on hot nights.
        It's a practice, they say,
        Which has not caused dismay,
    Except on some rather long flights.

XL

A SUSPICION OF SEX

A quick-thinking fellow called Fred
Leapt out of the marital bed
    With fine calculation
    Of ejaculation,
To roger the lodger instead.

A tongue-tied young fellow said, "Nell,
With you on my lap, I can't tell
    The thoughts I conceal
    Or just what I feel."
She told him, "I feel it as well."

A randy young fellow from Chard
Told women who squealed as he starred:
    "There's no need to shout
    When I put it about:
It isn't my hearing that's hard."

A chauvinist fellow called Stoker,
In bed with his wife, thought, "I'll poke her."
    He was heard to relate:
    "It really was great!
At one point, it damn' nearly woke her."

Jack said to his wife, "Listen, Jill,
If you manage an orgasm, will
    You make sure I know?"
    She answered, "Right-ho!"
And she did, in a phone call from Rhyl.

A Suspicion of Sex

Aged 90, Fred murmured, "I've based
My life on the women I've chased.
       Eighty years, I've pursued 'em
       And wooed 'em and screwed 'em.
The ten before that were a waste."

     In bed, Sharon said, "I suspect
     That a mirror up there's not correct.
         It shows me your bum
         As you come-come-come-come -
     And you don't give me time to reflect."

A satisfied lady called Bridget,
Whose man was a masterful midget,
       Said, "I've never yet failed
       To be thrilled when impaled
On his totally out-of-scale widget."

     When man finds the mate he's been hunting,
     They get down to groping and grunting.
         That's not what one sees
         With the birds and the bees:
     How on earth does a bee bonk a bunting?

Murmured Rex, "After sex, I can show it'll
Be fun on a run, even though it'll
       Be a dash around Salop -
       My own post-horn gallop:
Post-horn and post haste and post-coital."

     A slip of a thing had a nipper :
     She'd been plumbed by a passing day-tripper.
         She'd failed to decide
         Not to fall for the slide
     And the slip of a thing he would slip her.

A Suspicion of Sex

Though Sharon can sometimes be sniffy,
With airs just a little bit iffy,
   If she's out with a bloke
   And she fancies a poke,
She will tell him to slip her a stiffy.

JUST WILLY 'EM

**A gigolo known as Stud Dove
Has a quintet of willies for love.
   Other men's wives
   Just lie down in fives,
And his jeans seem to fit like a glove.**

**This fellow, a tar from the Scillies,
Is happy to boast of five willies.
   Other men's wives
   (Who lie down in fives)
Just wait to be told what the drill is.**

**The aforesaid young sailor (called Dove)
Always has a quintet to make love.
   Not one in three men
   Has such able semen
(Nor jeans which will fit like a glove).**

**The doc said, "Why, heaven's above!
A multiple line-up and shove!
   I see what the thrill is,
   Having five willies
(And jeans which just fit like a glove)."**

Said a free-loving lady in Chard,
"I am honest enough to regard
   My life as quite sleazy
   And virtue as easy,
Though what I attract is quite hard."

A Suspicion of Sex

Said a lecherous lad, "I depend
On a dink with the drive to extend,
    When I'm loving a lass,'
    Straight out through her ass,
With room on the end for a friend."

        Incest is what gives a mister
        A sexual life that's a vista
            Of straining relations
            And long explanations,
        And frequently boring his sister.

The earth moves for Karen and Paul -
A Richter-scale feel to it all:
        Seismological labours
        Annoying the neighbours,
Who frantically hold up the wall.

        A lecherous lady from Bude,
        With whom he had romped in the nude,
            Then denied their affair.
            He declared, "Don't despair:
        I'll think how to get you unscrewed."

Dawn's diet's effective but crude:
She says she can't eat when she's screwed.
        She has a good lay
        Just three times a day
Before meals. It's her F-Plan: no food.

        Sand, sun and sex! It imparts
        A thrill when a holiday starts.
            One finds it excites
            Those for whom it unites
        Gritty parts, foreign parts, private parts.

A Suspicion of Sex

A lady of limited passion
Resolved to put romps on the ration.
    She retained, as a rule,
    Her conjugal cool -
Then she'd rut in a rabbit-like fashion.

THE FELLOW FROM KENT

Remember that fellow from Kent,
Whose willy was withered and bent;
    Who saved himself trouble
    By going in double,
And thought he was coming but went?

Ladies, it can't be denied,
Simply sighed at his side-by-side slide.
    They, too, doubled up
    At the sight of his tup
And the room for another inside.

His strategy did not deceive
A lass whose inordinate sleeve
    Accepted his fiction
    But then found no friction.
She said, "It must stand up or leave."

It was sheer desperation when he
Tried folding his willy in three.
    Though direction was right,
    Penetration was slight
(Says a lady who sat up to see).

That push-it-in-double man (Kent),
Who thought he was coming, but went,
    Now clamps balls to tip
    With a jubilee clip -
Which helps, to a certain extent.

A Suspicion of Sex

The neighbours see life in the raw
When ladies arrive back for more
    Of the ploy they enjoy
    With a toy boy named Roy
In the service department next door.

    A girl he'd attempted to goose
    Soon opened her legs for his juice.
        There in the dark,
        He rose like a lark,
    Then shrivelled: he'd played fast and loose.

Said Fred, "Though you might not have guessed,
I don't plan a night on the nest.
    If it's hard as a rock,
    Spontaneous cock -
That's sperm-of-the-moment - is best."

    High noon, and two blowsy arousers
    Set caps at two drowsy carousers.
        At quarter to three,
        Complain of *ennui:*
    Carousers unroused, still in trousers.

A lad got his love life to prosper
With a sting on his ding from a wasp - a
    Hell of a shock,
    Augmenting his cock,
And swelling statistics at RoSPA.

    A slow-screwing lad from The Gower
    Was awash with young maids to deflower,
        But he'd find that he'd mind
        All the bind of a grind
    Every hour on the hour for an hour.

A Suspicion of Sex

Jane said to Linda, "Do you
And your husband speak during a screw?"
　　Linda said, with a groan,
　　"If he calls on the phone
When I'm at it, what else can we do?"

　　　Said Morag, "It's not done to brag
　　　Of a father who'll shag with a slag.
　　　　　It's a fag and a drag.
　　　　　I'm ignoring the bag
That Dad bagged in Baghdad, the hag."

Willies are Nature's conundrum.
When ladies are offered funundrum,
　　　They've the cheek to require
　　　Benefactors' desire
Be suppressed while they try to comundrum.

　　　　A carefully programmed analysis
　　　　Of the fun ladies offer for phalluses
　　　　　　Reveals that the arts
　　　　　　Polly plies with her parts
　　　　Are not as attractive as Alice's.

A wicked old reprobate played
His hand with a winsome young maid.
　　　With a face full of doom,
　　　Led her into his room.
The shag pile was specially laid.

　　　　A lad with unlimited zeal
　　　　Explained he had basic appeal
　　　　　　For molls wanting more:
　　　　　　He could do an *encore*
　　　　With a speed they agreed was unreal.

A Suspicion of Sex

The sex-bomb declared, "I make clear
To any young man who comes near,
    That he'll find that the grind
    I've refined is designed
To give him a tit in each ear."

    Their very first sexual connection
    Lacked aptitude, time and affection.
        In fleeting affinity,
        She lost her virginity,
    Her cool and all sense of erection.

Said Mary, "It's most impolite
That I should be screwed every night
    By a stranger who's sluiced,
    Who is not introduced,
And simply can't do the job right."

    A petulant lady from Ealing
    Said, "I don't feel that sex is appealing.
        I find that a grind
        Is a swine of a bind
    When I'm trying to look at the ceiling."

"Safe sex is the thing", declared Fred.
"It's a gospel I've constantly spread.
    Stay out of harm's way
    When making your play:
Have a rail that goes right round the bed."

    Said Sharon, while bonking with Wayne,
    Whom she'd met just that evening in Spain,
        "Aren't you going to come,
        Now we're having ho-hum?"
    To which he replied, "What, again?"

A Suspicion of Sex

A lass who was large and libidinous
Led lads to the last gasp of giddiness.
    At every encounter,
    Those ready to mount her
Faced slopes that were vast and vertiginous.

TWO OF A KIND

He said, as they strolled to the trees,
"No need to help me or tease.
    The speed I ejaculate
    Means you're on your bactulate."
She told him, "Just come as you please."

An eager young man from Belize
Makes love with his ladies in threes.
    He's no inhibitions
    Regarding positions,
And asks them to come as they please.

Though a mermaid, her chest undulating,
Is a minx when she thinks about dating,
    Any lad who should wish
    To deflower half a fish
May find he meets problems in mating.

Fred naturally never forgets
His train ride with two young nymphets.
    He found love was free
    In their shared *wagons lits.*
He calls them his double bonkettes.

A grateful young lady from Gloucester
Confided in friends that she'd loucester
    Compliant virginity
    To Michael the minity
Popped into bed to accoucester.

A Suspicion of Sex

A startled young lady from Leicester
Insisted that heaven had bleicester.
        In fact, her new baby
        Had started in Blaby,
The night that old Charlie careicester.

            You can't have a graceful orgasm.
            Apart from a muscular spasm,   ·
                    There are grunts, there are smells,
                    Then some horrid stuff gels.
            I've been told by a lady who hasm.

An impotent fellow called Fox
Turned to drink after sexual shocks.
        He said, "It's the norm
        That I fail to perform.
I need something stiff on the rocks."

            A lusty young lady said, "If
            I am bored, then the bore must be stiff.
                    With a wobble or bend,
                    I am at a loose end:
            That's a cock-up at which I just sniff."

A lively young lady named Lois
Was famed for her sexual prois
        And coital genius
        With all kinds of penius.
The snooker club said it with flois.

            "Not a thing", declared Fred, "could be finer
            Than to find that you're in Carolina.
                    Carolina's a lass
                    With a great little ass.
            I met her one night in a diner."

A Suspicion of Sex

Said a frantic young fellow called Izzy,
Who got the girls into a tizzy
By coming so quick
When they played with his dick,
"I can't wait: I am ever so busy."

TWO OF A KIND
A lad, whose assiduous dating
Failed to meet his requirements for mating,
Took his unfulfilled phallus
One day to the palace
And lit on a lady-in-waiting.

He was told by his mum that he shouldn't,
And told by his girl that he couldn't,
But his unfulfilled phallus
Was primed at the palace
By a lady-in-waiting who wouldn't.

Said an impotent fellow from Nantes
To a staid and dismayed maiden aunt,
"I always felt silly
With any young filly:
I wooed if she cooed, but I can't."

So why don't we make up a four
And double our chances to score?
Two girls and two jokers,
Four tits and two pokers -
Change ends at half time for some more.

An insatiable lady from Spain
Drove lots of her lovers insane.
When she felt a lad wilt
As his passion was spilt,
She cried, "Lovely! Now do it again!"

A Suspicion of Sex

Said a lusty young lady, "I find,
When entwined in a grind, I'm inclined
    To cry out, *'Again!'*
    But if they refrain
After only five times, I don't mind."

    A forceful young lady called Carole
    Was odd, both in lusts and apparel.
        A lover said later,
        "She dressed like a waiter
    And then had me over a barrel."

Said a lady of morals and charm,
"Perhaps if I stayed icy calm
    And did not do my nut,
    I could rut like a slut
And there'd not be a great deal of harm."

    The duchess found moments to treasure
    With a carrot that seemed made to measure.
        And the best of the joke
        Of this substitute poke -
    The foliage furthered her pleasure.

There's a lady who's widely desired,
Though her feelings aren't fired as required.
    She sleeps on the job,
    Ignoring the knob,
But her snorgasm's always admired.

    A raver called Beverley knew
    How to make love so cleverly, few
        Could match the elation
        She gave copulation -
    Without breathing heavily, too.

A Suspicion of Sex

When they'd bonked for a minute or two,
And she pined for the virtue she knew,
    He replied, "You're too late:
    You've been favoured by fate,
With a screw that you cannot undo."

    Sex was a joy he'd not known
    Until now, when the feeling had grown
        From primeval urge
        To glorious surge.
    It's a shame he was all on his own.

A scandalised lady from Wall
Complained, "All these stories are tall.
    It's insane and inept
    To suggest that I slept
With old Fred: I had no sleep at all."

    A laid-back young lady named Beverley
    Lay back for the lads rather cleverly.
        Their needs were all met,
        Though she never broke sweat,
    And she climaxed without breathing heavily.

A lusty young lady from Wigwig
(In Shropshire: it's not very bigbig)
    Met a lad of like mind
    And was happy to find
They'd soon settled down to some jigjig.

    Said a satisfied lady in bed,
    "Regarding my friendship with Fred:
        It started platonically,
        Just ginantonically.
    Never you mind where it's led."

A Suspicion of Sex

Fred never dallied or dithered.
If he spotted a slot, up he slithered.
    His excitable dick
    Meant he had to be quick,
Or before he had slithered, he'd withered.

    A lady of limited passion
    Proclaimed, "I've put bonks on the ration.
        It's a bind, but I find
        I'm inclined just to grind
    In resigned and refined kind of fashion."

Two couples - two men and their missuses
Are aware what the outcome of kisses is.
    They're intimate friends:
    Half-time, girls change ends,
To see what occurs for their clitorises.

    A leg-spreading lady from Leek
    Declared, "It's not profit I seek.
        Any fellow can see
        That what's in it for me
    Is simply himself, so to speak."

A virgin who sought to be sure
That she'd like a young man to imbue her,
    Went flat on her back
    For Fred, Bill and Jack,
But the standard of entry was poor.

    A libidinous lady who screwed
    From morning to night was quite shrewd.
        When she'd had her last lay,
        She'd be knackered and say,
    "Now I need my eight hours and some food."

A Suspicion of Sex

Fred's wife was cut quite to the quick
When she caught him in bed with a chick,
    She screamed, with a stare,
    "What y'doing in there?"
Said Fred, "There, I told you she's thick."

    An innocent laddie from Looe
    Always thought that a screw was a screw,
        So he'd pop in his prick,
        Spin clockwise quite quick,
    And enquire, "How is it for you?"

There's a fairly unfortunate chick
With a chap with a one-inch-long dick.
    But he does like his oats,
    And that's why she notes,
"Too little, too often, too quick."

    "Oral sex", Sharon said, "can't be right.
    At its best, it sounds most impolite.
        If it means what it's saying,
        Then Wayne will be praying
    I'll speak with my mouth full tonight."

The corporal declared, "I'm a soldier.
You'll find out, as soon as I holdier.
    My extra dimension
    Will spring to attention,
The minute I. . . there, now, I toldier."

    "No, don't wear a condom, please, Rex",
    She says, so the lad stops and checks,
        Stripped down to one sock:
        "This has come as a shock."
    "Here's another", she says. "There's no sex."

XLI
THE BOTTOM LINE

ON the day that young Mabel was wedded,
Some mesh in her bum got embedded.
　　It twangs like a harp,
　　She can fart in F sharp
And anything shitted is shredded.

　　A wickedly wonderful art
　　Is the silent and sulphurous fart
　　　　Which you leave in a left,
　　　　Inescapably sniffed,
　　A moment before you depart.

The trots? You have got 'em, that's clear:
A pitiless bottom, my dear -
　　　　A largely unspellable,
　　　　Not so unsmellable,
Super-dilute dire rear.

　　The effects of the trots are dismaying:
　　If you're wanting the loo - no delaying!
　　　　You live cheek-by-jowl
　　　　With a beast of a bowel
　　And a bottom that goes without saying.

Suppose you sat down for a shit: you-
'd be shocked if the roof fell from *situ*.
　　　　Go there again,
　　　　And it's perfectly plain:
The dare of the bog, sir, that hit you.

The Bottom Line

Evolution of Man (Chapter Two),
Adapting to things that are new:
    It sounds pretty heinous,
    A bayonet-fit anus,
With vacuum-assist on the loo.

    Why is always when you
    Are a visitor using the loo,
        That you turn out a turd
        That's obscene and absurd
    And refuses to flush out of view?

An *entrepreneur* once dismayed
The whole of the fizzy drinks trade.
    He agreed, "Though it's silly,
    I fart through my willy
And find that I pee lemonade."

    An apple-cheeked Irish colleen
    Explained, "I'm a farting machine."
        With decorous charm,
        She's become a wind farm
    And powers two-thirds of East Sheen.

An unspeakable odour once led
A council to act in some dread.
    It checked every sewer,
    Banned storing manure,
And found Fred had farted in bed.

    Fred's farts are so hard to believe:
    Keep everyone on the *qui vive*.
        Anatomical science
        Meets daily defiance:
    He's always got one up his sleeve.

The Bottom Line

It's a cert with the squits, when you've got 'em,
That you know that you're going to spot 'em,
    Since all of that shit
    Needs a bottomless pit
To cope with your pitiless bottom.

    A fed-up young fellow called Joe,
    Who grumbled that life was too slow,
        Concocted a brew -
        Senna pods, vindaloo,
    Prunes and figs - and soon found it all go.

Said Granny, who's really quite sweet,
As she lugged an old tyre up the street,
    "I'm terribly slow,
    But I don't want to know
What you catch from a lavatory seat."

    A bashful old man in Dunoon
    Is just like a captive balloon.
        Eighty years and not farted,
        So once he gets started,
    He'll blast himself straight to the moon.

Doing fart after fart, Fred inclines
To have anti-social designs
    And a burgeoning yen
    For scoring a ten.
So far, he has found beanz meanz neinz.

    Fred's personal time clock is fine:
    It's merely by freak of design
        That his bowel's in spate
        Each morning at eight,
    And he wakes at a quarter to nine.

The Bottom Line

At Fred's birth, his folks said, "We're not starting
With nappies for what he's imparting."
      He was ever so young
      When they fitted a bung,
And he's not found the pleasures of farting.

      Mother Nature quite soon got the hang
      Of designing a turd free of pang.
            It's great to depend
            On the point at the end,
      So your bum doesn't close with a bang.

Young Susan's most popular party act's
Breaking wind with unusual artefacts.
      Her skirts hide old boots,
      A jar and two flutes,
And produce unforgettable farty acts.

      You're all-over brown, but not well:
      The shit's hit the fan, we can tell.
            You're wishing, you mutt,
            You'd kept your mouth shut.
      And as for your smell - bloody hell!

The needs of his bowels had spurred him
To the off-putting gents where we heard him.
      But his meaningful moaning
      And grunting and groaning
Had clearly so far not deterred him.

      A well-trained young lad from East Sheen,
      Who shuts the loo lid, is quite keen
            That nobody knows
            The fact that he goes -
      Or what he has done when he's been.

The Bottom Line

We're certain that Fred's getting dafter.
He visits the loo, roars with laughter,
    Then does as he's bid
    And lowers the lid -
But does it before and not after.

    Said a lad from the village of Smite,
    "I find that when screwing, I shite.
        Propagating the species
        While covered in faeces,
    I ask, 'Am I doing this right?'"

Though your outlook on life may be sunny,
A shit while you screw isn't funny.
    A brown smelly worm
    Coincides with your sperm.
(It's possibly worse if it's runny).

    Constipation is anguish to man.
    To cure it, he does all he can.
        A turd then descends
        With a point at both ends
    And wraps·itself twice round the pan.

A lady who sat on the loo,
For a shit that was long overdue,
    Was foiled by a fart
    Which blew it apart.
She still hasn't done number two.

    Fred walked with his gait all askew -
    Mincing steps and with hips twisting, too.
        He explained, "It's a farce,
        Being fed through your arse,
    If you get a large toffee to chew."

The Bottom Line

. . . he's done it again!

The Bottom Line

They say natural gas has no smell -
A fallacy, as you can tell
    By merging a man
    With beans from a can
And letting the chemistry gel.

    An hour from the time that he'd started,
    The speaker said what he'd imparted
        Should make it all clear.
        Fred said, just to hear
    An arsehole, he'd rather have farted.

A tentative, useless young man
Attempted to goose his old gran.
    She said, "What a crass
    Way of feeling my ass!
Take advice from my son, your old man."

    When asked about mailing abroad,
    Old Joe simply nodded and roared:
        "Send her off like a parcel,
        With stamps on her arcel,
    Postcoded - and trust in the Lord."

There would be a profound diminution
In the world's atmospheric pollution
    If all of life's farters
    Would try, just for starters,
The cork-up-the-jaxi solution.

    On the phone to a friend, Sally Jane
    Said, "Roger's a regular pain.
        If I don't see him come,
        He goes straight for my bum,
    Then he'll. . . *Sod him! He's done it again!*"

OH, I SAY!!!

EXPLETIVES he uses are rather
Distinctive when he's in a lather:
        "Bloody hellfire
        And double-dyed mire
And how is your shit-sodden father!"

        "I've stopped nail-biting!" said Tess.
        "My fingers all looked such a mess.
                And now I've got claws,
                I'm receiving applause
        For picking my nose with *finesse*."

When a peer who's peeing appears
To peer to one side, it's to see - as
                His neighbour's urinal,
                Eight times out of ninal,
Show far more to pee with than he has.

        Said Sue, "In the sperm bank I give a
        Performance that makes the men quiver.
                To start with, I dress
                As Highwayman Bess,
        Then I strip and they stand and deliver."

From Wanda, a timely reminder:
You don't need to see, once you find her.
        With footnotes in Braille
        On her tits and her tail,
With your eyes closed, you still play a blinder.

Oh, I Say!!!

A man with a point on his penis
Missed out on the joys of his genus.
      He would say to some chick,
      "You will feel a small prick",
And then he went in, intravenous.

      A spinster recluse in a garret
      Once tried to make love with her parrot.
          When nothing occurred,
          She gave it the bird.
      She vegetates now, with a carrot.

Fred, high on a cliff-top, cried, "Shite!"
When she grabbed him and fell through the night.
      Though not her intention,
      His organ's dimension
Approximates Beachy Head's height.

      Big Donald is anxious to nab
      All the young girls he can grab.
          His best party trick
          Is five on his prick.
      He signs himself Don *à* Kebab.

A free-loving lady in Troon
Was seduced by a passing baboon.
      Her dalliance led
      To a monster she fed
By catapult, never a spoon.

      There's a social disease with a sting, as
      It takes time to come but it lingers:
          No cause for applause
          For messing with whores -
      Slow hand-clap, the pox of the fingers.

Oh, I Say!!!

"It's called conservation!" cried Wicket.
"With this hose up my nose, I can't pick it.
    The far end, I think,
    Will recycle drink.
I'll show you the place where I'll stick it."

    I had noticed a shortage of glee
    In the man sitting opposite me,
        And then I remembered
        I had seen him dismembered
    And hanged at a quarter-to-three.

A helpful young fellow from Brum
Made a fanny one day for a chum.
    It was shaped like a po,
    Making chum want to go,
And while he was going, he'd come

    Water is one of the few
    Of life's liquids I tend to eschew.
        It clears out a drain,
        Which makes me refrain,
    And goldfish all crap in it, too.

Though mean-minded men may go wooing,
Economies prove their undoing.
    Their curious tactics
    With used prophylactics
Consistently screw up their screwing.

    A lovely young widow in Tring
    Kept her late husband's ding on a spring.
        If it sprang with a twang,
        She would have a quick bang,
    While her friends gathered round in a ring.

Oh, I Say!!!

Fred said to the duchess, with force,
"I promise to work like a horse.
      But there, please depend,
      Similarities end:
You won't see my bollocks, of course."

      A lad whose incendiary dick
      Ignites on insertion quite quick,
          Is deft with a singe
          For a minge with a fringe:
      His comings and goings are slick.

Adultery brings to fruition
Explicit illicit coition.
      Her role is the hole
      For planting his pole,
And his is the sin of emission.

      Though flushing is vital for loos,
      The stalls in the gents don't amuse.
          What kind of a swine'll
          Design a urinal
      That pisses all over your shoes?

Said Joe, in the gents' for a pee,
To a peer who peered with some glee:
      "Don't be rude! You intrude!
      This is all I've accrued!
It's a joke - and it's privates to me!"

      Two Scotsmen debated with gravity
      The way their names hinted depravity
          When spoken in order
          Up North of the Border:
      First Ben Doon and then Phil McCavity.

Oh, I Say!!!

When soreness imposed a restriction
On the scope of her screwing addiction,
    She said with great glee
    That Castrol GT
Separated the act from the friction.

Sweet Kate thinks it's great to perform
On the loo something out of the norm.
    She will stand on the seat,
    Put her head on her feet,
And pee 'til the cistern gets warm.

My favourite farts, now I note 'em,
Are the silent compressed ones: I vote 'em
    My best fun for weeks,
    As I sit, clenching cheeks,
And feel them go *phut!* past my scrotum.

New glasses! Wet trousers! Dismay!
See everything twice! That's OK!
    But I piss in the sink,
    See two dinks and I think
One's not mine, so I put it away.

A condom is something to doff
When you've just finished having it off,
    Or else you will see,
    In the gents when you pee,
That it swells, slips and plops in the trough.

A thoughtful young thing called Rebecca
Was distraught upon growing a pecker.
    Though she knew what to do
    When she went for a poo,
We could see her split pee would soon wreck her.

Oh, I Say!!!

There is a young fellow named Nick,
Who is blessed with an air-controlled prick.
    The girls are ecstatic
    When shafted pneumatic,
But the hiss with his piss makes them sick.

    There's a worried young man who is sick
    Whenever he puts in his prick.
        He explains that the spewing
        That goes with the screwing
    Can distract a slick chick from his dick.

A flatulent floozie from Eltham,
Whose farts laid you out if you smeltham,
    Would trap you in bed,
    With her tits round your head,
And you'd not leave alive 'til you'd feltham.

    A floozie zoologist's habit,
    With a chance of some sex, was to grab it.
        Her elasticised crack
        Was just right for a yak,
    A rhino, a wren or a rabbit.

A free-thinking guy in The Gower
Explains self-adornment adds power.
    That ring through his cock,
    Though a bit of a shock,
Lets him hang the shampoo in the shower.

    There's a long-fingered fellow in Ealing,
    Whose courting is most unappealing.
        The girls never stay
        To have it away,
    Explaining they've had a gut feeling.

Oh, I Say!!!

Cried a fellow, while waving his dick,
"This isn't a new kind of trick.
    I'm not being rude
    Or incredibly crude:
I'd just like this mousetrap off, quick."

    The stomach's the way, we admit,
    To reach a man's heart. (It's a bit
        Anatomically strange
        That the route we arrange
    With a woman is through her left tit).

A laboratory lass called Louise
Keeps dozens of dicks in deep freeze.
    She explains, "They perform
    Very well with a warm,
And better, if given a squeeze."

    "If a man should attack me", said Julie,
    "You won't have to worry unduly.
        The yell that there'll be
        Will be his, not from me.
    It will mean that I'm chewing a goolie."

There is a young lady who's peed
On her garden for years, killing weed,
    Ending plague, pest and drought -
    But it's really about
Fulfilling her own urgent need.

    Fred's quite clearly caught Nature napping,
    With his bowel and his cock overlapping.
        He'll not only shit
        When he's having a bit:
    He comes when his bum's busy crapping.

INDEX OF FIRST LINES

A dissatisfied lady in Bloxwich	The National Health
Adultery brings to fruition	Oh, I Say!!!
Advocates of PC thought we might	Imperfectly Correct
A farmer enjoyed the Bahamas	Life on the Land
A farmer who sat on his ass	Life on the Land
A fart with too much compressed air	Religious Disorders
A fed-up young fellow called Joe	The Bottom Line
A fellow called Cook got quite used	First Impressions
A fellow whose cock catches fire	Merely Males
A feminist tart of great flair	The Oldest Profession
A fencing contractor did well	Occupational Hazards
A fish in a bowl is a farce	Animal Antics
A flat-chested duchess who's witless	The World of Words
A flat-chested lass from Valletta	Shall We Join the Ladies?
A flatulent fellow called Geoff	A Little Learning
A flatulent floozie from Eltham	Oh, I Say!!!
A flatulent nun, Sister Clare	Religious Disorders
A flatulent oaf made a start	All for Art
A floozie zoologist's habit	Oh, I Say!!!
A foolish young fellow from Bude	Merely Males
A footman said, "Nothing compares	Occupational Hazards
A forceful young lady called Carole	A Suspicion of Sex
A former car driver named Russ	A Message Mistaken
A forthright young fellow in Dorking	First Impressions
A frantic young fellow from Dorset	Slightly Saucy
A free-loving lady in Troon	Oh, I Say!!!
A free-thinking guy in The Gower	Oh, I Say!!!
A freezing young tart, playing sentry	The Oldest Profession
A frisky young fellow called Price	The Oldest Profession
After crying, "Free will is for all!"	A Message Mistaken
A furtive and brief stolen kiss	Slightly Saucy
A gardener based on a theory a	Religious Disorders
A gay wing three-quarter called Joe	Sporting Gestures
Age before beauty is neat	The World of Words
Aged 80, Fred cried, "Life can fill me	Slightly Saucy
Aged 90, Fred murmured, "I've based	A Suspicion of Sex
Aged six, Fred was painful to watch	Sporting Gestures
A ghostly philanderer called Sam	A Chance of a Ghost
A gigolo known as Stud Dove	A Suspicion of Sex

A girl he'd attempted to goose	A Suspicion of Sex
A grateful young lady from Gloucester	A Suspicion of Sex
A gratified lady from Stoke	Slightly Saucy
A great tit exclaimed, "It's absurd!	Animal Antics
A greedy young fellow from Delph	The National Health
A gut-bucket sighed, "Being round	Love's Labour's Lost
A handsome young dentist in Gillingham	The National Health
A handsome young gentleman, built	The World of Words
A handsome young man from Darjeeling	The National Health
A hardly-inhibited whore	The Oldest Profession
A haulage contractor's wife, Nan	A Message Mistaken
A healthy young priest says repression	Religious Disorders
A helpful young fellow from Brum	Oh, I Say!!!
A helpful young hooker called Fay	The Oldest Profession
A helpful young lass from Devizes	Slightly Saucy
A high-wire walker knows dire	Occupational Hazards
A hit of a miss called Miranda	Religious Disorders
A hooker who's also a cook	The Oldest Profession
A hopeful young surgeon called Todd	The National Health
A horrified son of the soil	The National Health
A hospital doctor looked glum	The National Health
A keeper of bees came to grief	Occupational Hazards
A knight, while crusading in Palma	Occupational Hazards
A laboratory lass called Louise	Oh, I Say!!!
A labourer down in The Weald	A Suspicion of Sex
A laddie who's very well built	Merely Males
A lad got his love life to prosper	A Suspicion of Sex
A lad who does musical farts	Musical Items
A lad who had gone round the bend	Merely Males
A lad who made love in a camper	The World of Words
A lad, whose assiduous dating	A Suspicion of Sex
A lad whose incendiary dick	Oh, I Say!!!
A lad with a laughable dong	Merely Males
A lad with a laughable penis	Merely Males
A lad with a lusty *libido*	Merely Males
A lad with a prehensile poker	Merely Males
A lad with unlimited zeal	A Suspicion of Sex
A lady accustomed to cocks	The Oldest Profession
A lady of limited passion *(2 verses)*	A Suspicion of Sex

A lady who lounged in the nude	First Impressions
A lady who sat on the loo	The Bottom Line
A lady whose limit was two	The Demon Drink
A lady who shops in the nude	Logical Lapses
A lady who showed great resource	Lawful Occasions
A lady who's living in sin	The Demon Drink
A lady who's lovely, though large	Signs of Uncertainty
A laid-back young lady named Beverley	A Suspicion of Sex
A lap-dancing club is a place	Slightly Saucy
A lascivious lady for whom	The Oldest Profession
A lass who was large and libidinous	A Suspicion of Sex
A lecherous lady from Bude	A Suspicion of Sex
A lecherous poltergeist hid	A Chance of a Ghost
A leg-spreading lady from Leek	A Suspicion of Sex
A lesbian said, "It's a shock to me	The National Health
A letters exchange is the way	The World of Words
A liberal Ms (not a Mrs)	Imperfectly Correct
A libidinous lady who screwed	A Suspicion of Sex
A lively young lady named Jane	Love's Labour's Lost
A lively young lady named Lois	A Suspicion of Sex
A lonely young man from The Gower	Domestic Issues
A lovely young girl at De Witts	Slightly Saucy
A lovely young Swedish au pair	First Impressions
A lovely young widow in Tring	Oh, I Say!!!
Alphabetically speaking, you may	The World of Words
Although Fred called Fifi *très bonne*	Love's Labour's Lost
Although test tube babies aren't rare	The National Health
A luminous condom's decreed	Domestic Issues
A lush of a lady called Queenie	The Demon Drink
A lusty young lady from Wigwig	A Suspicion of Sex
A lusty young lady said, "If	A Suspicion of Sex
A male ballet dancer's no chump. He	All for Art
A male ballet dancer wears gear	All for Art
A man with a point on his penis	Oh, I Say!!!
A man with a very long beast	A Very Long Thing
A man with a very long chopper	A Very Long Thing
A man with a very long cock	A Very Long Thing
A man with a very long dibber	A Very Long Thing
A man with a very long dick	A Very Long Thing

A man with a very long dickie	A Very Long Thing
A man with a very long dink *(2 verses)*	A Very Long Thing
A man with a very long dong *(3 verses)*	A Very Long Thing
A man with a very long end *(2 verses)*	A Very Long Thing
A man with a very long friend	A Very Long Thing
A man with a very long hampton	A Very Long Thing
A man with a very long heinie	A Very Long Thing
A man with a very long jack	A Very Long Thing
A man with a very long jizzy	A Very Long Thing
A man with a very long jobby	A Very Long Thing
A man with a very long member	A Very Long Thing
A man with a very long part	A Very Long Thing
A man with a very long pecker	A Very Long Thing
A man with a very long peg	A Very Long Thing
A man with a very long phallus	A Very Long Thing
A man with a very long pleaser	A Very Long Thing
A man with a very long plonker	A Very Long Thing
A man with a very long pole *(2 verses)*	A Very Long Thing
A man with a very long prick	A Very Long Thing
A man with a very long rivet	A Very Long Thing
A man with a very long rod	A Very Long Thing
A man with a very long snake	A Very Long Thing
A man with a very long tadger	A Very Long Thing
A man with a very long thing	A Very Long Thing
A man with a very long tiggy	A Very Long Thing
A man with a very long tine	A Very Long Thing
A man with a very long todger	A Very Long Thing
A man with a very long tool *(3 verses)*	A Very Long Thing
A man with a very long totem *(2 verses)*	A Very Long Thing
A man with a very long weapon	A Very Long Thing
A man with a very long whang *(5 verses)*	A Very Long Thing
A man with a very long willy *(3 verses)*	A Very Long Thing
A man with a very long wire	A Very Long Thing
A man with a whang with a bend	Merely Males
A man with the smallest of ends	Merely Males
A matron whose humour was raw	The National Health
A mellow young fellow in Spello	All for Art
A mini-dinked fellow called Trevor	Love's Labour's Lost
A misogynist Welshman called Bryn	Religious Disorders

A novice was somewhat dismayed	Religious Disorders
An unspeakable odour once led	The Bottom Line
A one-legged workman from Wick	Sporting Gestures
a over *b*, in coition	A Little Learning
A Parisian actor called Alec	Correspondence Course
A *pas de deux's* clearly rehearsed	All for Art
A passionate couple in Yonkers	TheWorld of Words
A patient vouchsafed with dismay	The National Health
A peculiar title is Brit	The World of Words
A penniless Scotsman called Rob	The World of Words
A perfect young gent, when in drink	The Demon Drink
A petulant lady from Ealing	A Suspicion of Sex
A pig farmer living near Fareham	Life on the Land
A plantsman got up people's noses	The Oldest Profession
A plonker-proud fellow called Roy	Slightly Saucy
A plonker-proud fellow told Sue	First Impressions
A pools coupon madam and whores	The Oldest Profession
A poor little fellow called Morgan	The World of Words
A postman who screws in full livery	Occupational Hazards
A punter felt rather a prat	The Oldest Profession
A quick one-night stand can be hell	Love's Labour's Lost
A quick-thinking bridegroom called Ted	Marriage Lines
A quick-thinking fellow called Fred	A Suspicion of Sex
A raddled old tart said, "I find	The Oldest Profession
A randy bisexual punk	Religious Disorders
A randy gargantuan Greek	Love's Labour's Lost
A randy Red Indian chief	Slightly Saucy
A randy young fellow called Sean	Merely Males
A randy young fellow from Chard	A Suspicion of Sex
A randy young fellow from Kent	Love's Labour's Lost
A randy young poet from Hay	Literary Leanings
A rather deaf farmer called Heep	A Message Mistaken
A rather large lady, inclined	Shall We Join the Ladies?
A raver called Beverley knew	A Suspicion of Sex
A really quite rude Grenadier	First Impressions
A ribald young poet from Tring	Literary Leanings
A rugger lad's lass said, "No wonder	Sporting Gestures
A sailor from South Tyne and Wear	Occupational Hazards
A sailor in search of some yo-ho	The Oldest Profession

A salesperson answered an ad	Imperfectly Correct
A sassy young lassie named Jacquelyn	Shall We Join the Ladies?
A satisfied lady called Bridget	A Suspicion of Sex
A scandalised lady from Wall	A Suspicion of Sex
A Senegal girl thought it odd	The World of Words
A sex-mad soprano in Devon	Occupational Hazards
A sex-starved young lady named Kay	Slightly Saucy
A shag-happy celibate said	The World of Words
A Shakespeare thesp from Crickhowell	All for Art
A shapely young shopgirl called Jude	Slightly Saucy
A *ship for men* - did you know?	Anarchic Anagrams
A signwriter, thinking he knew it all	Signs of Uncertainty
A slip of a thing had a nipper	A Suspicion of Sex
A slow-screwing lad from The Gower	A Suspicion of Sex
A songstress who did it for fun	Musical Items
A spinster recluse in a garret	Oh, I Say!!!
As Spooner (the Rev) was a hit	Religious Disorders
A starlet explained she had barred a	One for the Road
A startled young lady from Leicester	A Suspicion of Sex
A stripper's act got out of hand	Occupational Hazards
A student of maths, with a sigh	A Little Learning
A stylish young lady named Heather	Occupational Hazards
A surgeon whose home was in Filey	The National Health
At a concert, a fellow called Jones	Musical Items
A tart in Boulogne, name of Fleur	The Oldest Profession
A tart with her cleft in her head	The Oldest Profession
A teacher of maths in Rouen	A Little Learning
A tennis girl's fans were unnerved	Sporting Gestures
A tentative, useless young man	The Bottom Line
At Fred's birth, his folks said, "We're not starting	The Bottom Line
At Graceland, a groupie's one sentence	A Chance of a Ghost
A theatregoer, while canned	The Demon Drink
At home or in far distant lands	Slightly Saucy
A thoughtful transsexual said, "Nurse!	Reversals
A thoughtful young fellow named Mark	One for the Road
A thoughtful young thing called Rebecca	Oh, I Say!!!
A thoughtful young thing in Dundee	Shall We Join the Ladies?
At mental arithmetic, few	A Little Learning
A tongue-tied young fellow said, "Nell	A Suspicion of Sex

At the mission, the lovely Shefali	Religious Disorders
At the trade fair, old Chatburn looked glum	Signs of Uncertainty
A vampire dressed as a toff	A Message Mistaken
A very tall warder who knew	Lawful Occasions
A virgin who sought to be sure	A Suspicion of Sex
A well-built young lady called Kay	Shall We Join the Ladies?
A well-endowed gay says it's true	Slightly Saucy
A well-endowed lady from Gwent	Shall We Join the Ladies?
A well-endowed lady in tears	Sporting Gestures
A well-endowed lady who's rudish	Slightly Saucy
A well-hung young fellow from Ealing	Merely Males
A well-hung young man from Carlisle	Slightly Saucy
A well-stacked young dancer named Joan	Occupational Hazards
A well-trained young lad from East Sheen	The Bottom Line
A whorehouse allotment caused doubts	The Oldest Profession
A whore in a harem in Suez	The Oldest Profession
A whore in the desert admitted	The Oldest Profession
A wickedly wonderful art	The Bottom Line
A wicked old reprobate played	A Suspicion of Sex
A wizened old spinster who knew	The World Of Words
A woman soon grows to depend	Slightly Saucy
A yeast-and-hops addict called Kay	The Demon Drink
A young cockerel said, "It's dismayed me	Animal Antics
A young Irish lawyer called Thomas	Lawful Occasions
A young keep-fit novice in Brum	The World of Words
A young lady cried, "I'm bereft!	Shall We Join the Ladies?
A young lady harpist from Rio	Musical Items
A young racing driver said part	Sporting Gestures
BABES? Sperm, if we really believe 'em	Slightly Saucy
Batsmen are often a failure	Sporting Gestures
Behind a young lady, old Jack	A Message Mistaken
Being deaf, and with strange peccadilloes	Literary Leanings
Bewildered psychiatrists speak	Shall We Join the Ladies? ·
Big Donald is anxious to nab	Oh, I Say!!!
Birth Announcements clerk brought Mum to tears	A Message Mistaken
Birthday suits give a chance of comparing	Merely Males
Boadicea, charioteer, no mistaking	Just Back in Time
Bookshops have such a collection	A Little Learning

211

But then, with a trollop named Sue	Merely Males

C̸ALLING actresses actors, though silly — Imperfectly Correct
Celibate - haven't you heard? — The World of Words

Cold weather unfailingly knocks	Merely Males
Compatible seems the right label	Domestic Issues
Conservationist Samuel, a builder	Occupational Hazards
Conservation's concerns were extended	Anarchic Anagrams
Constipation is anguish to man	The Bottom Line
Crappy Rubsniff! You're left in the dark?	Reversals
Cried Adam, "I've seen in a vision	Biblical Bits
Cried a fellow, while waving his dick	Oh, I Say!!!
Cried a grateful young man from East Sheen	Slightly Saucy
Cried a lass who would strip but not tease	Slightly Saucy
Cries Paddy, with something that juts	Merely Males
Curvaceous young ladies are full	The World of Words

D̸IY gynaecologists all — The National Health
DNA, sad to say, intervenes — The National Health

David Mellor could not be ignored	Anarchic Anagrams
Dawn's diet's effective but crude	A Suspicion of Sex
Dear Billy, Although I've no doubt	Correspondence Course
Dear Daughter, I don't give a damn	Correspondence Course
Dear Mary, I have to agree	Correspondence Course
Dear Mum, Life at college is swell	Correspondence Course
Dear Mummy, How can I begin	Correspondence Course
Dear Son, It's a hoot, you'll agree	Correspondence Course
Dear Steve, Can't believe that you're serious	Correspondence Course
Dear Trace, When we bonk, you will curse if I	Correspondence Course
Desmond Tinnie, a sculptor in Epsom	Occupational Hazards
Despite what some expert decides	A Little Learning
Dirty jokes have no future at all	The World of Words
Disinfectant would shoot from Fred's dink	Merely Males
Doing fart after fart, Fred inclines	The Bottom Line
Don't rhyme me with *moon, June* or *spoon!*	Slightly Saucy
Don't scoff at my lack of virility!	Merely Males
Don't the judges who laughingly say	Lawful Occasions

E̸MBRYOLOGY can, it's reported — The National Health
Eros, it's clear, knows the score — The World of Words

G AND S, you might guess, were aglow — Anarchic Anagrams
Genealogy fascinates some — Shall We Join the Ladies?
Geography's dealt me a blow — A Little Learning
Girls with *panache* are the best — Slightly Saucy
Gondoliers (with a definite article) — Anarchic Anagrams
"Good morning, I'm Fred: who are you? — First Impressions
Gratified ladies know when — Slightly Saucy

HANDS-ON is the method of healing — The National Health
"Hello! You're a nympho, they claim — First Impressions
He produced with a flourish and pride — Love's Labour's Lost
Here's a thought which may possibly pain us — A Little Learning
Her laden butler shocked the Lady Sybil — Occupational Hazards
Her lover was always demonic — Love's Labour's Lost
He romped with Penelope, founding — Slightly Saucy
He said, as they strolled to the trees — A Suspicion of Sex
He says, "One, two, three" and can score — Love's Labour's Lost
He was told by his mum that he shouldn't — A Suspicion of Sex
He yawned and replied with a grin — Merely Males
Hey diddle diddle, the cat — Cursory Nursery
High noon, and two blowsy arousers — A Suspicion of Sex
Him Tarzan? We doubt it a bit — Anarchic Anagrams
His complaint is quite likely to pain us — A Person from Brum
His problem will not be refuted — The Demon Drink
His strategy did not deceive — A Suspicion of Sex
Home schooling is very effectual — A Little Learning
How puzzling Nature can be! — The Oldest Profession

I came, saw and conquered. Proclaim — Just Back in Time
"If a man should attack me", said Julie — Oh, I Say!!!
If anything's hard to forgive, it is — Domestic Issues
If his willy won't rise, there's dismay — Anarchic Anagrams
If you fart on TV, you can tell — The Media
If your tongue isn't slick, don't say quickly — A Slip of theTongue
Ignoring the clothes and the clamour is — Slightly Saucy
I had noticed a shortage of glee — Oh, I Say!!!
"I'm dreadfully sorry", Fred cried — Life on the Land
I'm musically out in the cold — Musical Items
In a greengrocer's shop in the region — Signs of Uncertainty

In a haunted old house on the coast	A Chance of a Ghost
In a longest-cock contest at Clee	Slightly Saucy
In bed in the dark, Fred had grown	Domestic Issues
In bed, Sharon said, "I suspect	A Suspicion of Sex
Incest is what gives a mister	A Suspicion of Sex
Increasing the world's population	A Little Learning
Initiative? Always a bit	The World of Words
In ladies' and gents', we can see	Slightly Saucy
In new lodgings, a randy old queen	A Message Mistaken
Interrupting the act has a fault	The World of Words
In the bathroom, the duke had a fit	A Slip of the Tongue
In the hay in the barn in the yard	Life on the Land
In the street, a young fellow called Gus	A Message Mistaken
In vain, she had sat on the loo	The World of Words
I require a concise explanation	A Little Learning
I saw one while out on a visit	Domestic Issues
I suggested a *ménage à trois*	Love's Labour's Lost
I think we should all raise our glasses	Signs of Uncertainty
It's a cert with the squits, when you've got 'em	The Bottom Line
It's always a sad little scene	Domestic Issues
It's a sign of the times, and it shows	Signs of Uncertainty
"It's called conservation!" cried Wicket	Oh, I Say!!!
It's Fred who will frequently hold	Fred
It's horses for courses, they say!	Sporting Gestures
It's no shock that a call girl named Alice's	The Oldest Profession
It sounds just a bit like hard porn	Cursory Nursery
"It's the blind man!" The call was a bind	A Message Mistaken
It was sheer desperation when he	A Suspicion of Sex
"I've gone blind!" exclaimed old Mrs Brown	A Message Mistaken
"I've stopped nail-biting", said Tess	Oh, I Say!!!
ACK", murmured Jill, hasn't mastered	The Demon Drink
Jack pulled, with a finger and thumb	A Message Mistaken
Jack said to his wife, "Listen, Jill	A Suspicion of Sex
Jack-the-lad knew he had to come clean	One for the Road
Jane knows intuition is right	A Message Mistaken
Jane said to Linda, "Do you	A Suspicion of Sex
Jill's honeymoon hopes had been heightening	Marriage Lines
Just WHY did that bishop of Birmingham	Religious Disorders

LADIES, it can't be denied	A Suspicion of Sex
Limericks, from time immemorial	Literary Leanings
Little Bo is a scurrilous creep	Cursory Nursery
Little Red Riding Hood's meeting	Cursory Nursery
Lusting lads always wanted to meld 'em	Anarchic Anagrams
MAKE a farce of your art - that's the way	All For Art
"Make your bids!" said the man with the mike	A Message Mistaken
Male strippers are left in a daze	Occupational Hazards
Manchester finds with a start	Reversals
Many a lad is a wannabe	The World of Words
Marco Polo, it seems, was a chap	Anarchic Anagrams
Medical shorthand is very	The National Health
Midsummer Night's Dream is the play	Literary Leanings
Miss Howard asked, "Is this the norm?"	The World of Words
Missionaries have recognition	Religious Disorders
Miss Muffet declared, looking glum	Cursory Nursery
Monica said, "I concede a	Just Back in Time
Mother Nature quite soon got the hang	The Bottom Line
Mrs Crapper's inaugural piddle	Logical Lapses
Murmured Rex, "After sex, I can show it'll	A Suspicion of Sex
"My boy friend has habits", said Rhoda	One for the Road
My favourite farts, now I note 'em	Oh, I Say!!!
My highly intelligent dog	Animal Antics
NEW glasses! Wet trousers! Dismay!	Oh, I Say!!!
No danger you might drop a clanger	The Oldest Profession
"No, don't wear a condom, please, Rex	A Suspicion of Sex
No lady would call Fred a liar	Love's Labour's Lost
No man, so they say, is an island	Slightly Saucy
"Not a thing", declared Fred, "could be finer	A Suspicion of Sex
No woman's been known to refuse	The World of Words
No wonder a cockerel's not staid	Animal Antics
OH, doctor!" cried Fred, "it's not right	The National Health
"Oh, heavens! I've stepped on your dong!"	Slightly Saucy
Old Harold believes diabetes	Old Harold
Old Harold believes diarrhoea	Old Harold
Old Harold believes that short-sighted	Old Harold
Old Harold believes time and motion	Old Harold

Old Harold, on elbows and knees	Old Harold
Old Harold's a pain when he's pissed	Old Harold
Old Harold's now drawing his pension	Old Harold
Old Harold's technique is quite handy	Old Harold
Old Harold these days tends to make	Old Harold
Old Harold tried hard to explain	Old Harold
On American freeways, the art	Signs of Uncertainty
One of life's little delights	Slightly Saucy
One way that such verses will rivet is	Literary Leanings
On the day that young Mabel was wedded	The Bottom Line
On the hearthrug in front of the Baxi	Love's Labour's Lost
On the phone to a friend, Sally Jane	The Bottom Line
"On this", Jack declared, "please depend	The World of Words
"Oral sex", Sharon said, "can't be right	A Suspicion of Sex
P*AT on back for Eighth Army* - a brief	The Media
People know a young fellow called Nick	A Message Mistaken
Pete's perpendicular dick	Merely Males
Pisa's queer tower was designed	A Little Learning
Pop singers have trouble requiting	Musical Items
Possessive wife, mother of two	Correspondence Course
Precisely at quarter-to-two	The World of Words
Prince Chas, with great brass, spoke of bed	Slightly Saucy
Propped up in his bed, Fred will start	The National Health
Puffed Thor, "I'd have been quite a prat if I'd	A Message Mistaken
Purveyors of pop somehow bring	Musical Items
R ELIGION is what's always stirred	Religious Disorders
Remember that fellow from Kent	A Suspicion of Sex
Repetitive metrical flow	A Health Warning
"Reproduction's a word, murmured Jane	The World of Words
Rome's burning and there in the middle	Musical Items
Rotten Haystacks contrived to supply	Introduction
Rowing's a curious sport: a	Sporting Gestures
S ADO-MASOCHISTS' odd little ways	Merely Males
"Safe sex is the thing", declared Fred	A Suspicion of Sex
Said a big-mouth who'd just had a date	Slightly Saucy
Said a bimbo, while looking the part	Slightly Saucy

Said a bishop, while having a pee	Religious Disorders
Said a bishop who bonked, "I'm a blighter	Religious Disorders
Said a bishop who strayed, "I declare, it	Religious Disorders
Said a blonde, "I'm a lesbian who	A Message Mistaken
Said a blushing young man from Devizes	First Impressions
Said a builder, while working in Chard	Occupational Hazards
Said a bustard, "It's plain to discern	Animal Antics
Said a carpenter, seeking some twine	A Message Mistaken
Said a celibate cricketer who	The World of Words
Said Adam, when in at the birth	Biblical Bits
Said a duchess with spots on her bottom	Animal Antics
Said a duck, with a cluck, "I don't stress it	Animal Antics
Said a flat-chested lady from Stroud	Shall We Join the Ladies?
Said a floozie called Susie, "Although	The Oldest Profession
Said a floozie called Susie, "I've faced	The Oldest Profession
Said a Ford Transit driver named Dan	Occupational Hazards
Said a frantic young fellow called Izzy	A Suspicion of Sex
Said a free-loving lady in Chard	A Suspicion of Sex
Said a frugal young lady from Maine	The Demon Drink
Said a groper who groped in Valletta	Slightly Saucy
Said a highly frustrated young gent	Love's Labour's Lost
Said a lad from the village of Smite	The Bottom Line
Said a lad who had lost his *élan*	Love's Labour's Lost
Said a lad with *libido* fixation	The National Health
Said a lad with no balls, "None's enough, as	Merely Males
Said a lady, both wiser and older	Love's Labour's Lost
Said a lady, "It's safer to doodle	Animal Antics
Said a lady of morals and charm	A Suspicion of Sex
Said a lady who, feeling quite flirty	A Message Mistaken
Said a lady who sat on a flute	Shall We Join the Ladies?
Said a lady who sought to divorce	Occupational Hazards
Said a large, almost globular man	Love's Labour's Lost
Said a lecherous lad, "I depend	A Suspicion of Sex
Said a lusty young lady, "I find	A Suspicion of Sex
Said a maiden from South Borehamwood	Slightly Saucy
Said a maid with a mountainous chest	Shall We Join the Ladies?
Said a man with two willies and stubble	Merely Males
Said a marketing girl, name of Nelly	The Media
Said a masochist psychic, "My rule is	A Chance of a Ghost

218

Said a middle-aged mermaid on waking — Shall We Join the Ladies?
Said an anxious young man from Belize — Merely Males
Said an anxious young man in Torquay — Merely Males
Said a naturist golfer from Tring — Sporting Gestures
Said an elderly spinster called Mabel — A Message Mistaken
Said an impotent fellow from Nantes — A Suspicion of Sex
Said an odious fellow from Crewe — The World of Words
Said an old window cleaner one day — Occupational Hazards
Said a pensive young thing in Valletta — Love's Labour's Lost
Said a porky young lady, "I sweat — Shall We Join the Ladies?
Said a priest, "I am celibate, faced — The World of Words
Said a raddled old tart, "I protest — The Oldest Profession
Said a raddled old tart, "Nothing rocks — The Oldest Profession
Said a rancher, "I have a strange fear — Life on the Land
Said a randy old canon, "The wits — Religious Disorders
Said a satisfied lady in bed — A Suspicion of Sex
Said a satisfied lass, with a wink — Shall We Join the Ladies?
Said a sheepish young sheila from Oz — Sporting Gestures
Said a tart who was trading as Annie — The Oldest Profession
Said a wayward old bishop one night, "E- — Religious Disorders
Said a wine buff, "My piles are just fine — The Demon Drink
Said a wistful old man in Dunoon — Merely Males
Said a young mum, when out with her brood — Domestic Issues
Said Fifi, "With bondage. I've found — The Oldest Profession
Said Fred, "I'd find sex more appealing — Love's Labour's Lost
Said Fred, "I do not think it wise — Merely Males
Said Fred, "I love Mother, but such — Domestic Issues
Said Fred, in the gents' for a pee — A Message Mistaken
Said Fred, "I've no wish to intrude — First Impressions
Said Fred, "Though I think she's *très bong* — Slightly Saucy
Said Fred, "Though you might not have guessed — A Suspicion of Sex
Said Fred, "What's the point of denial? — Signs of Uncertainty
Said Granny, who's really quite sweet — The Bottom Line
Said Harold, "The trouble with sex — Old Harold
Said Jack, "Do you think we should sort of — Love's Labour's Lost
Said Jane, on the phone to a chum — Love's Labour's Lost
Said Janet, "You cannot deny — Slightly Saucy
Said Jock, "As a cock, it's just fine — Merely Males
Said Joe, in the gents' for a pee — Oh, I Say!!!

219

Said Liszt to his friend, "I've no qualms	Musical Items
Said Morag, "It's not done to brag	A Suspicion of Sex
Said Mary, "It's most impolite	A Suspicion of Sex
Said Sharon, "Although your intention	Love's Labour's Lost
Said Sharon, while bonking with Wayne	A Suspicion of Sex
Said Sue, "In the sperm bank I give a	Oh, I Say!!!
Said Sue to her husband, "It's true	Domestic Issues
Said Susie, "I cannot be thrilled	Love's Labour's Lost
Said Susie, "I've never denied	Shall We Join the Ladies?
Said the actress, "My lord, that was fine	Religious Disorders
Said the canon, "I'd always desired	Religious disorders
Said the doctor, "I trust you won't mope	Merely Males
Said the duchess, "I hear oarsmen share	Sporting Gestures
Said the Heir to the Throne, who was seen	A Message Mistaken
Said the tart, "From the start, to be blunt	The Oldest Profession
Said the vicar, "I'm now realising	Religious Disorders
Said Tracy, whose lad was a copper	Lawful Occasions
Sand, sun and sex! It imparts	A Suspicion of Sex
Santa's been heard to complain	Occupational Hazards
Sarah Ferguson sure didn't give a damn	Anarchic Anagrams
Say police, who've increasingly been	Lawful Occasions
Scruple's a word that is full	The World of Words
Seeking thrust for his marital art	Love's Labour's Lost
Sex is so short; what is more	The World of Words
Sex-mad but sterile, she hired	The World of Words
Sextuplets born in Samoa	Slightly Saucy
Sex was a joy he'd not known	A Suspicion of Sex
Sharon gives sex a new angle	Shall We Join the Ladies?
She cried, "Mother's milk is the best!	Domestic Issues
She said that his willy was vast	Love's Labour's Lost
She said, with a coy little grin	A Message Mistaken
Sighed Jill, "Well, the doctor who's seen us	Love's Labour's Lost
Sister Clare, with a coy little snigger	Religious Disorders
Six damsels, each draped in a duster	Slightly Saucy
Sobbed the duke, "I have had such a fright!	Slightly Saucy
So Blodwen is marrying Josh!	Marriage Lines
Solemnity was the main feature	First Impressions
Some ghostly and randy hillbillies	A Chance of a Ghost
Some happy old girls in the Gower	Slightly Saucy

223

There was a young man from Clovelly	There Was a. . .
There was a young man of Qatar	There Was a. . .
There was a young miss from Torbay	There Was a. . .
There was a young person from Brum *(8 verses)*	A Person from Brum
There was a young thing from St Mawes	There Was a. . .
There was a young woman from Diss	There Was a. . .
There wath a young lath called Thamantha	Slightly Saucy
There would be a profound diminution	The Bottom Line
The *R* has been changed to a *P*	Signs of Uncertainty
These saucy adventures he's led	Fred
These verses, you may have inferred	Introduction
The sex-bomb declared, "I make clear	A Suspicion of Sex
The smile of the coy Mona Lisa	All for Art
The sport that absorbed Aberystwyth	Slightly Saucy
The stomach's the way, we admit	Oh, I Say!!!
The tasteless is clearly no bar	Anarchic Anagrams
The trots? You have got 'em, that's clear	The Bottom Line
The young lady gasped, "That's a whopper!"	Slightly Saucy
They're monsters that make people stare	Shall We Join the Ladies?
They say natural gas has no smell	The Bottom Line
They've said to Ezekiel, "Come off it!"	Biblical Bits
This fellow, a tar from the Scillies	A Suspicion of Sex
This time around, you are faced	Introduction
Those who resort to coition	A Little Learning
Though a mermaid, her chest undulating	A Suspicion of Sex
Though a surgeon named James is quite dim	The National Health
Though flushing is vital for loos	Oh, I Say!!!
Though his willy was widely admired	Merely Males
Though mean-minded men may go wooing	Oh, I Say!!!
Though Sharon can sometimes be sniffy	A Suspicion of Sex
Though your outlook on life may be sunny	The Bottom Line
Throughout *A Midsummer Night's Dream*	Literary Leanings
Time after time, he's awoken	Love's Labour's Lost
Tina's tennis has earned her renown	Sporting Gestures
To a randy archbishop's delight	Religious Disorders
"To lose armpit hair", said Gervaise	A Message Mistaken
To slow down the mad speeding chumps	Signs of Uncertainty
To travel by post, for a jest	Slightly Saucy
Turd is a word that is ripe	The World of Words

Two call girls at lunch, to unwind	The Oldest Profession
Two couples - two men and their missuses	A Suspicion of Sex
Two fatties felt Nature was mocking	Love's Labour's Lost
Two gardeners, Plantem and Pickem	A Message Mistaken
Two glasses of brandy are handy	The Demon Drink
Two lads sat on spikes on a wall	The National Health
Two nuns caused a stir at the fete	Religious Disorders
Two nuns, Sisters Mercy and Jo	A Message Mistaken
Two Scotsmen debated with gravity	Oh, I Say!!!
Two sex theory courses last winter	A Little Learning
Two well-endowed pranksters on Sark	Slightly Saucy
UNTHANKED, Mother Nature imparts	Merely Males
WAITER! You haven't a clue!	Logical Lapses
Water is one of the few	Oh, I say!!!
Wee Jean of the generous orifice	The Oldest Profession
"Well, well!" said the vice girl, "That's nice!	The Oldest Profession
We're certain that Fred's getting dafter	The Bottom Line
West Ham, Crystal Palace - a sparse	Sporting Gestures
Whatever makes hedgehogs decide	Animal Antics
What kindness is Nature bestowing	The World of Words
When a full house hears Hamlet intone	Literary Leanings
When a peer who's peeing appears	Oh, I Say!!!
When a punter had died on the job	The Oldest Profession
When asked about mailing abroad	The Bottom Line
When asked, "Do you smoke while you screw?"	The Oldest Profession
When cattle swim rivers, it's clear	Animal Antics
When Charlie ran off with a cow	Animal Antics
When does man start to show some good breeding?	Merely Males
"When Fred's will is read", people said	Lawful Occasions
When in Cornwall and too full of whisky	The World of Words
"When I pee", Fred declared, "I discern	Merely Males
When Jill climbs the hill, without fail	Cursory Nursery
When Jock dropped his trousers, the shock	Domestic Issues
When man finds the mate he's been hunting	A Suspicion of Sex
When soreness imposed a restriction	Oh, I Say!!!
When tarts in Madrid take a stroll	Signs of Uncertainty

When they'd bonked for a minute or two .... A Suspicion of Sex
When told that Fred's bathroom was pink .... A Message Mistaken
Why is it always when you .... The Bottom Line
Willies are Nature's conundrum .... A Suspicion of Sex
Wind-breaking acts, it's admitted .... The Media
With agencies' learning the art .... Slightly Saucy
With a howl of dismay, Charlie's daughter .... Shall We Join the Ladies?
With a late urge to breed like a rabbit .... Religious Disorders
With a mixed-doubles lady from Wall .... Sporting Gestures
With an honesty long overdue .... The World of Words
With a rectal inspection to come, it a- .... The National Health
With his hands in his crotch, there was Jack .... A Message Mistaken
With Walkman, all hope disappears .... Merely Males

YOU can't have a graceful orgasm .... A Suspicion of Sex
You keep two-in-one verse alive .... The World of Words
Young Sharon keeps causing hilarity .... Slightly Saucy
Young Susan's most popular party act's .... The Bottom Line
Young women, quite oddly, decide .... Marriage Lines
You're all-over brown, but not well .... The Bottom Line
Your name, little dog, is so apt! .... Animal Antics

* * *